First published in the UK in 2000 by Earthscan Publications Ltd

ISBN: 1 85383 730 X

Printed and bound in the UK by Thanet Press
Substantive editing, design, and prepress production by Communications Development in Washington, DC,
with art direction by its UK partner, Grundy & Northedge
Data and maps on pages 34–37 provided by IWMI, www.iwmi.org

Earthscan Publications Ltd
120 Pentonville Road
London, N1 9JN, UK
Tel: +44 (0)20 7278 0433
Fax: +44 (0)20 7278 1142
Email: earthinfo@earthscan.co.uk
http://www.earthscan.co.uk

Earthscan is an editorially independent subsidiary of Kogan Page Ltd and publishes in association
with WWF-UK and the International Institute for Environment and Development

This book is printed on elemental chlorine-free paper

world WATER
vision

Making Water Everybody's Business

William J. Cosgrove and Frank R. Rijsberman
For the World Water Council

**World
Water
Vision**

**World
Water
Council**

**Conseil
Mondial
de l'Eau**

EARTHSCAN
Earthscan Publications Ltd, London

Word from the President of the World Water Council

Water is life, in all forms and shapes. This basic yet profound truth eluded many of us in the second half of the 20th century. Water professionals and scientists around the world were ringing the alarm bells of an impending water crisis. Yet attempts to address some of the issues or to offer partial solutions met with limited success.

As the world population increased and urbanisation and industrialisation took hold, the demand for water kept rising while the quality continued to deteriorate. Water scarcity afflicted many more nations, and access to clean drinking water and sanitation remained poor. A decline in public financing and a rise in transboundary water conflicts made these problems worse. But awareness of the problems was limited to the few on the "inside," in the water sector. We start the new century with a water crisis on all accounts. A concerted effort and extraordinary measures are needed to face the challenges head on.

From its inception the World Water Council has understood the dimensions of the world water crisis. The Council realized that a first step towards solving this crisis is the development of a shared vision on world water for the long term. The *Long Term Vision for Water, Life, and Environment in the 21st Century*—or World Water Vision, for short—was introduced during the World Water Council's first World Water Forum in Marrakech, Morocco, in 1997. The Marrakech Declaration gave the Council the mandate to develop such a Vision. Planning and preparation went at full speed in 1997 and 1998. By the summer of 1998 preparation of the Vision commenced in earnest.

This Report is the culmination of the Vision development exercise. The monumental work was carried out under the direct responsibility of William J. Cosgrove, director, and Frank R. Rijsberman, deputy director, of the Vision Management Unit, World Water Council. We are very grateful for their tireless efforts, patience, perseverance, and diligence in managing, synthesising, and editing this text.

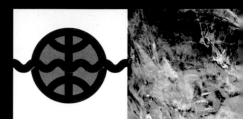

The World Water Council also acknowledges the tremendous support and exceptional contribution to the development of the World Water Vision by staff of the Vision Management Unit, members of the Vision Management Committee of the World Water Council, members of the Thematic and Scenario Panels, and members of the World Commission on Water for the 21st Century—the World Water Commission—and its senior advisors.

Special thanks go to Ismail Serageldin for chairing the World Water Commission and for mobilising resources and the media in support of the Vision. This work would not have been possible without the generous financial support of the government of the Netherlands. Our gratitude also goes to Bert Diphoorn, Koos Richelle, and their colleagues at the Ministry of Foreign Affairs. We acknowledge the excellent service and support provided by the Water Science Division of the United Nations Educational, Scientific, and Cultural Organization for hosting the Vision Management Unit. Many other organisations made financial, intellectual, and other contributions to the Vision, and their contributions are much appreciated.

It is not possible to list here all those who contributed professionally and with devotion to the World Water Vision. Their enthusiasm and dedication make this work a unique contribution in the history and development of the world's water resources.

This work is dedicated to the children of the world, because we did not inherit the world from our parents—we borrowed it from our children.

Mahmoud A. Abu-Zeid
President of the World Water Council
Minister of Water Resources and Irrigation
Giza, Egypt

Word from the Chairman of the World Water Commission

Yes, water is life. Every human being, now and in the future, should have enough clean water for drinking and sanitation, and enough food and energy at reasonable cost. Providing adequate water to meet these basic needs must be done in an equitable manner that works in harmony with nature. For water is the basis for all living ecosystems and habitats and part of an immutable hydrological cycle that must be respected if the development of human activity and well-being is to be sustainable.

We are not achieving these goals today, and we are also on a path leading to more crises and problems for a larger part of humanity and many more parts of the planet's ecosystems. Business as usual leads us on an unsustainable and inequitable path.

To address these issues, the World Water Council convened a World Commission on Water for the 21st Century—or World Water Commission, for short—that was cosponsored by all the United Nations agencies working on water and development. I have had the privilege of chairing this distinguished Commission. I have also had the privilege of working with an excellent team, the Vision Management Unit of the World Water Council, headed by two remarkable individuals, the authors of this Report.

The World Water Vision exercise, carried out under the guidance of the World Water Commission, has involved many thousands of women and men in an extraordinary participatory exercise over an 18-month period. These people contributed to an unprecedented effort to increase awareness of the water crisis that affects billions of people already. More than 40 groups of people around the world have worked on the development of their visions of sustainable management of water in their region or sector. Their reports are published separately. Together all these people will not only increase worldwide water awareness, but will also shape public policy on water in the 21st century.

This Report is the tip of the iceberg. It reflects the visions of many in a single, global statement. I commend the authors. They did a superb job of producing four rapidly evolving versions of the World Water Vision in an open, transparent process through which hundreds of people reviewed their drafts and provided extensive comments. Even more, they were the engine behind the Vision exercise, shaping the process, raising funds, motivating people to participate, and believing—as I did—that the impossible ought to be done in just 18 months.

This Report and the many associated documents that it draws on were essential inputs into the deliberations of the World Water Commission and in the formulation of the recommendations contained in the Commission's report. *World Water Vision: Making Water Everybody's Business* is timely. It is authoritative. And I am convinced that it will contribute to changing our world water future.

Ismail Serageldin
Chairman
World Water Commission on
Water for the 21st Century

Contents

Figures, Tables, and Boxes

Preface

In recent years it has become evident that there is a chronic, pernicious crisis in the world's water resources. Participants at the first World Water Forum—held in Marrakech, Morocco, in 1997 and sponsored by the World Water Council—called for a World Water Vision to increase awareness of the water crisis and develop a widely shared view of how to bring about sustainable use and development of water resources. The World Water Council responded and developed the World Water Vision as its main programme.

The World Water Vision draws on the accumulated experience of the water sector, particularly through sector visions and consultations for Water for People (Vision 21; WSSCC 1999), Water for Food and Rural Development, Water and Nature, and Water in Rivers. Professionals and stakeholders from different sectors have developed integrated regional visions through national and regional consultations covering Arab countries, Australia and New Zealand, Baltic states, Canada, Central America and the Caribbean, Central Asia, China, the Danube Basin, the Mediterranean basin, the Nile basin, North America, the Rhine basin, South America, South Asia, Southeast Asia, Southern Africa, and West Africa. In addition, there were special projects on Interbasin Water Transfers; River Basin Management; A Social Charter for Water, Water, Education; and Training, Water and Tourism; and Mainstreaming Gender Issues.

The participatory process that led to the World Water Vision makes it special. Since 1998 some 15,000 women and men at the local, district, national, regional, and global levels have shared their aspirations and developed strategies for the sustainable use and development of water resources. The Internet made these consultations possible in a short timeframe. As the Vision evolved, more networks of civil society groups, nongovernmental organisations (NGOs), women, and environmental groups joined the consultations that influenced this Report. The diverse backgrounds of participants—authorities and ordinary people, water experts and environmentalists, government officials and private sector participants, academics and NGOs—offered a wide range of views. So, this is not an academic exercise—it is the start of a movement.

The participatory consultations will continue at the Second World Water Forum, being held at The Hague in March 2000. Many of the participants in the Vision exercise will have the chance to meet thousands of other interested stakeholders, including ministers from most countries, to discuss the solutions proposed in this Report and in dozens of other documents prepared as part of the Vision process. Over the coming months and years participants from the forum will develop action plans to implement the recommendations of the World Water Commission and the strategies herein.

The World Water Vision hopes to inspire women and men to overcome obstacles and achieve fundamental changes. Its message is for everybody—particularly the leaders and professionals who have the power and knowledge to help people turn visions into reality. It challenges those directly affected by the water crisis to initiate action and to call on their leaders to bring about sustainable water resource use and development.

The Vision recognises that people's roles and behaviours must change to achieve sustainable water resource use and development. The main actors will be individuals and groups in households and communities with new responsibilities for using water and water-related services. Public authorities will need to empower and support them and carry out work that households and communities cannot manage for themselves. Water professionals and environmentalists will provide these stakeholders with the information they need to participate in decisionmaking and will help implement their decisions. Working together, these groups can achieve this Vision.

World Water Vision: Making Water Everybody's Business, prepared by the staff of the Water Vision Unit for the World Water Council, complements the many documents being published by sector and regional consultation groups. It synthesises many findings, bringing together water issues on a global scale. (The analytical parts are published separately in a document called *World Water Scenarios: Analysis*.) The Vision exercise involved thousands of people

over an 18-month period. Women and men from around the world have participated in hundreds of meetings to formulate and discuss their local, national, regional, and sector visions for water in the 21st century. This Report is based on the visions developed in those consultations, on the documents generated by this process, and on the feedback and comments received. A listing of the partner organisations and some of the meetings, along with an overview of the background documents, is provided in the appendix.

The World Water Commission's report, signed by its members, also draws on many of these findings and exercises. But it is independent, and does not constitute a summary of these efforts. The positions on what constitutes a desirable future for water use and development at the global level, as contained in its report, were determined by the Commission in meetings at The Hague on 29–30 November 1999. This Report is intended to be consistent with the Commission's recommendations.

The analysis of current and future water resource availability and use described in chapters 2 and 3 is based largely on the work of the Scenario Development Panel (see appendix) and the modellers of the International Water Management Institute in Colombo, Sri Lanka; the International Food Policy Research Institute in Washington, D.C.; the Centre for Environmental Systems Research of the University of Kassel in Germany; the Stockholm Environment Institute, Sweden; and the Russian State Hydrological Institute in St. Petersburg. In addition, sector and regional vision documents were the sources for many boxes and analyses throughout the Report (see appendix).

The Global Water Partnership (GWP) was the key partner in the World Water Vision exercise. During the fist phase the GWP strongly supported the Vision exercise through regional committees that became the coordinators and facilitators of regional vision consultations. During

the second phase the GWP's parallel program, the Framework for Action, worked alongside the Vision exercise, took over the initiative in regions, and began to prepare action plans to achieve the Vision through a process called From Vision to Action.

William J. Cosgrove

Frank R. Rijsberman

Acknowledgements

This report went through four drafts, and many people provided more than two hundred extensive and thoughtful comments on these drafts, either as individuals or as representatives of their organisations: Jamal M. Abdo, National Water Resources Authority, Yemen; Anil Agarwal, Centre for Science and Environment; Tony Allan, School of Oriental and African Studies, University of London; Dogan Altinbilek, Ministry of Energy, Turkey; Arthur J. Askew, World Meteorological Organization; Milan Bedrich, Danube River Basin Programme; Patricio Bernal, United Nations Educational, Scientific, and Cultural Organization–Intergovernmental Oceanographic Commission; Janos Bogardi, United Nations Educational, Scientific, and Cultural Organization–International Hydrological Programme; Malia Bouayad-Agha, Vision Unit; Lucinda Boyle, Irrigation Association; John Briscoe, World Bank; Stefan Bruk, United Nations Educational, Scientific, and Cultural Organization; Margaret Catley-Carlson, World Water Commissioner; Bertrand Charrier, Green Cross International; H. Slimane Cherif, International Atomic Energy Agency; Rene Coulomb, Suez Lyonnaise des Eaux; Piers Cross, United Nations Development Programme–World Bank Water and Sanitation Program; Jean Dausset, Academie de l'Eau; Dick de Jong, International Water and Sanitation Centre; Roger de Loose, Rotary International; Charles-Lois de Maud'huy, Generale des Eaux (Vivendi); Wolfram Dirksen, German Association for Water Resources and Land Improvement; Victor Dukhovny; Farouk El-Baz, Boston University; Alan Ervine, University of Glasgow; Walter Falcon, Stanford University; Malin Falkenmark, Stockholm International Water Institute; Constantino A. Fasso, International Commission on Irrigation and Drainage; Stephen Foster, International Association of Hydrology; Jennifer Francis, International Water and Sanitation Centre; Luis Garcia, Inter-American Development Bank; Gouri Shankar Ghosh, United Nations Children's Fund; John Gladwell, Hydro Tech. International; Stela Goldenstein, Scenario Development Panel; Vincent Gouarne, World Bank; Biksham Gujja, World Wide Fund for Nature; Joyeeta Gupta, Free University, the Netherlands; Lilian Saade Hazin, International Institute for Infrastructural, Hydraulic and Environmental Engineering; Danielle Hirsch, Both ENDS; Howard Hjort, Food and Agriculture Organization; John Hodges, U.K. Department for International Development; Richard Holland, World Wide Fund for Nature; Constance Hunt, World Wide Fund for Nature; Ahmad Hussein, United Nations Educational, Scientific, and Cultural Organization, Malaysian delegation; Annelie Joki-Hubach, Both ENDS; Torkil Jonch-Clausen, Global Water Partnership–Technical Advisory Committee; Thomas M. Kimmell, Irrigation Association; Jean-Marcel Laferriere, Canadian International Development Agency; Raymond Lafitte, International Hydropower Association; Jacques Lecornu, International Commission on Large Dams; Guy LeMoigne, Senior Advisor, World Water Commission; Roberto Lenton, United Nations Development Programme; Stephen Lintner, World Bank; Robert Lytle, CH2M HILL; Chandra Madramootoo, McGill University; Ruth Meinzen-Dick, International Food Policy Research Institute; Mac Mercer, World Conservation Union; Doug Merrey, International Water Management Institute; Tony Millburn, International Water Association; Hans Mobs; Fernando Perez Monteagudo, Center for Hydraulic Research, Cuba; Chris Morry, World Conservation Union; P. Mosley; M. Edward Muckle, Green Resources Management Ltd.; Masahisa Nakamura, Lake Biwa Research Institute; Riota Nakamura, Japanese Institute of Irrigation and Drainage; Jean-Pierre Nicol, Association Francaise pour l'Etude de l'Irrigation et du Drainage; Hideaki Oda, Water for Rivers; Toshio Okazumi, Vision Unit; I.H. Olcay Unver, Southeastern Anatolia Project, Turkey; Rolph Payet, Ministry of Environment and Transport, Seychelles; Sandra Postel, Global Water Policy Project; Lin Pugh, International Information Centre and Archives for the Women's Movement; Amreeta Regmi, United Nations Development Fund for Women, South Asia; Peter Rogers, Harvard University; Salman Salman, World Bank; Barbara Schreiner, Ministry of Water Affairs and

Forestry, South Africa; Michael Schur; Senior Advisors, Water World Commission; John Soussan, University of Leeds; Hilary Sunman, Global Water Partnership Framework for Action Unit; Mark Svendsen, Water for Food; Henri Tardieu, Association Francaise pour l'Etude de l'Irrigation et du Drainage; Task Force of the Chief Executive Officer C.D. Thatte, International Commission on Irrigation and Drainage; Cecilia Tortajada, Third World Centre for Water Management; M.J. Tumbare, Zambezi River Authority; Rene Urien, Agricultural and Environmental Engineering Research, France; Isabel Valencia, Scenario Development Panel; Hans van Damme, Water Supply and Sanitation Collaborative Council; Jan Peter van der Hoek, Amsterdam Water Supply; Barbara van Koppen, International Water Management Institute; Frank van Steenbergen, Global Water Partnership Framework for Action Unit; Christine van Wijk, International Water and Sanitation Centre; Linden Vincent, Wageningen Agricultural University; Wendy Wakeman, World Bank; Water and Nature Team, World Conservation Union; Ranjith Wirasinhar, Water Supply and Sanitation Collaborative Council; and Paul Wolvenkamp, Both ENDS. While all the individuals listed provided valuable comments and corrections, they have not endorsed the Report, and all remaining errors and omissions are the responsibility of the authors. This report benefitted from the editing, design, and prepress production of Communications Development's Bruce Ross-Larson, Meta de Coquereaumont, Terry Fischer, Paul Holtz, Damon Iacovelli, Megan Klose, Daphne Levitas, and Molly Lohman and the art direction of Grundy & Northedge.

The start-up of the World Water Vision exercise and its continuation were assured by major financial support from the Ministry of Foreign Affairs of the Netherlands, particularly through the unfailing efforts of Bert Diphoorn. Additional funding for the exercise was pledged on short notice as the process moved forward. Since early 1999 other organisations have provided financial assistance, particularly the Swedish International Development Authority, Canadian International Development Agency, and Global Environment Facility. Finland, Luxembourg, and Switzerland have also contributed support. Many other organisations have contributed indirectly—for example, through the Global Water Partnership—or contributed time and resources in kind. The World Water Vision Unit has been the guest of the United Nations Educational, Scientific, and Cultural Organization's International Hydrological Programme at its headquarters in Paris.

In an undertaking as large as the World Water Vision exercise, made possible on short notice thanks only to the tireless efforts of many people, it is impossible to properly acknowledge and thank everyone for their contributions. An overview has been provided here and in the appendix, but to all who contributed and cannot find their name, an apology—as well as a heartfelt thank you!

e.

**Making Water
Everybody's
Business**

There is a water crisis today. But the crisis is not about having too little water to satisfy our needs. It is a crisis of managing water so badly that billions of people—and the environment—suffer badly

All life on earth has depended on water since the first single-cell organisms appeared 3.5 billion years ago—consuming energy, growing, reproducing. From that time until very recently in geological history, there was a balance between the needs of life and the available water. Humans appeared as a species less than 100,000 years ago. Sometime less than 10,000 years ago we developed stone tools, learned that we could cultivate our own food instead of just gathering it, established civilisations, and began migrating long distances.

In the past 200 years our numbers grew exponentially—more people to be fed, and more water needed by each person for economic development. In the past 100 years the world population tripled, but water use for human purposes multiplied sixfold! Today perhaps half of all available freshwater is being used for human ends—twice what it was only 35 years ago. Looked at another way, all freshwater serves human needs, because ecosystems provide goods and services to humanity beyond the obvious water for drinking, food production, and industrial uses. Think of the fish we eat, the benefits we enjoy from natural flood protection, and the water quality brought by healthy, functioning aquatic ecosystems.

Today's water crisis—and tomorrow's

There is a water crisis today. But the crisis is not about having too little water to satisfy our needs. It is a crisis of managing water so badly that billions of people—and the environment—suffer badly.

The most obvious uses of water for people are drinking, cooking, bathing, cleaning, and—for some—watering family food plots. This domestic water use, though crucial, is only a small part of the total (box 1). Worldwide, industry uses about twice as much water as households, mostly for cooling in the production of electricity. Far more water is needed to produce food and fibre (cereals, fruits, meat, cotton). We are not sure how much water

Executive Summary

Providing six times more water now than 100 years ago has significant impacts on people and the environment

- Green water—the rainfall that is stored in the soil and evaporates from it—is the main source of water for natural ecosystems and for rainfed agriculture, which produces 60% of the world's food.

- Blue water—renewable surface water runoff and groundwater recharge—is the main source for human withdrawals and the traditional focus of water resource management.

- The blue water available totals about 40,000 cubic kilometres a year. Of this, an estimated 3,800 cubic kilometres, roughly 10%, were withdrawn (diverted or pumped) for human uses in 1995.

- Of the water withdrawn, more than 2,000 cubic kilometres are consumed. The remainder is returned, usually with significant reductions in quality.

Not all renewable water resources are usable

- Of global water resources, a large fraction is available where human demands are small, such as in the Amazon basin, Canada, and Alaska.

- Rainfall and river runoffs occur in large amounts during very short periods, such as during the monsoon season in Asia, and are not available for human use unless stored in aquifers, reservoirs, or tanks.

- The withdrawal and consumption figures do not show the much larger share of the water resources "used" through degradation in quality—polluted and of lower value downstream.

- Water not used by humans generally does not flow unused to the sea. Instead it is used in myriad ways by aquatic and terrestrial ecosystems—forests, lakes, wetlands, coastal lagoons.

And:

- Even though people use only a small fraction of renewable water resources globally, the fraction is much higher in many arid and semi-arid river basins where water is scarce.

- In many tropical river basins a large amount of water is available only for short periods, so either it is not usable or massive infrastructure is required to store it for later use, with considerable social and environmental impacts.

- In many temperate zone river basins adequate water resources are distributed fairly evenly over the year but used so intensively that surface and groundwater resources become polluted and good-quality water becomes scarce.

Source: World Water Vision staff.

must remain in our ecosystems to maintain them, but indications are that we are approaching—and in many places have surpassed—the limits of how much water we can divert.

Providing six times more water now than 100 years ago has significant impacts on people and the environment. The cup is half full:

- A major investment drive, the International Drinking Water Supply and Sanitation Decade (1981–90) and its follow-up—led by national governments and supported through international organisations—ended with safe and affordable drinking water for 80% of the exploding world population and sanitation facilities for 50%.

- Major investments in wastewater treatment over the past 30 years have halted the decline in—even improved—the quality of surface water in many developed countries.

- Food production in developing countries has kept pace with population growth, with both more than doubling in the past 40 years.

- In perhaps the biggest achievement of the century, rising living standards, better education, and other social and economic improvements have finally slowed population growth.

But it is also half empty:

- An unacceptably large part of the world population—one in five—does not have access to safe and affordable drinking water, and half the world's people do not have access to sanitation. Each year 3–4 million people die of waterborne diseases, including more than 2 million young children who die of diarrhoea.

- More than 800 million people, 15% of the world population and mostly women and children, get less than 2,000 calories a day. Chronically undernourished, they live in permanent or intermittent hunger.

- Much economic progress has come at the cost of severe impacts on natural ecosystems in most developed and transition economies. Half the world's wetlands were destroyed in the 20th century, causing a major loss of biodiversity. Many rivers and streams running through urban centres are dead or dying. Major rivers—from the Yellow River in China to the Colorado in North America—are drying up, barely reaching the sea.

- Water services—irrigation, domestic, and industrial water supply, wastewater treatment—are heavily subsidised by most governments. This is done for all the right reasons (providing water, food, jobs) but with perverse consequences. Users do not value water provided free or almost free—and so waste it. Water conservation technologies do not spread. Incentives for innovation remain weak.

● Unregulated access, affordable small pumps, and subsidised electricity and diesel oil have led to overpumping of groundwater for irrigation and to drops in groundwater tables of several metres a year in key aquifers. As much as 10% of global annual water consumption may come from depleting groundwater resources.

● In most countries water continues to be managed sector by sector by a highly fragmented set of institutions. This system is ineffective for allocating water across purposes, precludes effective participation of other stakeholders, and blocks integrated water resource management.

The conclusion: while much has been achieved, today's water crisis is widespread. Continuing current policies for managing water will only widen and deepen that crisis.

What business as usual portends: severe stress

Because of population growth, the average annual per capita availability of renewable water resources is projected to fall from 6,600 cubic metres today to 4,800 cubic metres in 2025. Given the uneven distribution of these resources, some 3 billion women and men will live in countries—wholly or partly arid or semi-arid—that have less than 1,700 cubic metres per capita, the quantity below which people start to suffer from water stress. Also by 2025 an estimated 4 billion people, or more than half the world population, will live in countries where more than 40% of renewable resources are withdrawn for human uses—another indicator of high water stress under most conditions.

Under business as usual, with present policies continuing, economic growth to 2025 in developed and transition economies tends to increase water use. But this increase can be offset by efficiency improvements and the saturation of water demands in industry and households. In addition, the amount of irrigated land stabilises, and water for irrigation is used more efficiently. As a result total water withdrawals can—and should—decline. Extrapolating current trends of water quality does not present a rosy picture, however.

In developing countries higher incomes and increased access lead to greater household water use per capita, multiplied by the greater number of people. Meanwhile, economic growth expands electricity demand and industrial output, leading to a large increase in water demanded for industry. Even though water may be used more efficiently in households and industry, increased use overwhelms these improvements. Providing food to the growing population and ending hunger remain the largest challenge in the quantities of water demanded. The result is a projected large increase in water withdrawals in the agricultural, industrial, and domestic sectors of the developing world.

Adding together the trends in developed and developing countries under business as usual increases global water withdrawals from 3,800 cubic kilometres in 1995 to 4,300–5,200 cubic kilometres in 2025. The difference largely depends on how much irrigated agriculture does or does not expand.

This increase in water withdrawals implies that water stress will increase significantly in more than 60% of the world, including large areas of Africa, Asia, and Latin America. Will this lead to more frequent and more serious water crises? Assuming business as usual: yes.

Moving from crisis to Vision

Whether the water crisis deepens and intensifies—or whether key trends can be bent towards sustainable management of water resources—depends on many interacting trends in a complex system. Real solutions require an integrated approach to water resource management.

Crucial issues that may provide levers for very different futures include:

● Limiting the expansion of irrigated agriculture.

● Increasing the productivity of water.

● Increasing storage.

● Reforming water resource management institutions.

● Increasing cooperation in international basins.

● Valuing ecosystem functions.

● Supporting innovation.

Executive Summary

The more food we produce with the same amount of water,
the less the need for infrastructure development,
the less the competition for water, . . .

Table 1 Renewable water use in the World Water Vision

In our Vision the water for irrigated agriculture is drastically limited, with 40% more food produced (partly from rainfed agriculture) consuming only 9% more water for irrigation. Industrial use goes down in developed countries, but the decline is more than offset by increases in the developing world. Municipal use goes up sharply in developing countries, to provide a minimum amount for all, and down in the developed world. Recycling and increased productivity lower the ratio of water withdrawn to water consumed for all uses.

| | Cubic kilometres | | Percentage increase |
User	1995	2025	1995–2025
Agriculture			
Withdrawal	2,500	2,650	6
Consumption	1,750	1,900	9
Industry			
Withdrawal	750	800	7
Consumption	80	100	25
Municipalities			
Withdrawal	350	500	43
Consumption	50	100	100
Reservoirs (evaporation)	200	220	10
Total			
Withdrawal	3,800	4,200	10
Consumption	2,100	2,300	10
Groundwater			
overconsumption	200	0	

Source: Table 4.1.

In the World Water Vision the increase in water use for irrigated agriculture has to be drastically limited, with 40% more food produced (partly from rainfed agriculture) but only 9% more water consumed for irrigation (table 1). A significant decline in industrial water use in developed countries is more than offset by increases in the developing world. Municipal use goes up sharply in developing countries, to provide a minimum amount for all, and down in the developed world. Recycling and higher productivity reduce the amount of water withdrawn to meet consumption needs for all uses.

Limiting the expansion of irrigated land

The rate of expansion of irrigated land is the most important determinant of water stress, at least the stress related to quantity. There are two contrasting views on how the trend in irrigated agriculture's expansion will continue or bend, with important stakeholders weighing in on both sides.

The conventional wisdom in agriculture, based on the need to produce food for the growing world population, is that irrigated agriculture will have to keep pace—and therefore expand by 20–30% in area by 2025. The other perspective—supported by environmentalists and by some stakeholders in agriculture—holds that a slowdown in dam building and irrigation investments, combined with the consequences of dropping groundwater tables, will limit the expansion in irrigated area to 5–10%.

Neither alternative is attractive:

● *Unattractive alternative 1.* A 30% increase in irrigated area would require major investments in water infrastructure, a large portion of which would have to involve large dams. There would likely be severe water scarcities—and serious risks of deteriorating ecosystems.

● *Unattractive alternative 2.* A strong reduction in irrigation expansion—under otherwise unchanged policies, or business as usual—will cause considerable food shortages and rising food prices.

Both alternatives—each unattractive and unsustainable—would considerably deepen today's water crisis. So there is every motivation to implement policies that make food production and water resource management more sustainable.

. . . the greater the local food security, and the more water remains for household and industrial uses. And the more that remains in nature

Making water more productive: more crop per drop

The more food we produce with the same amount of water, the less the need for infrastructure development, the less the competition for water, the greater the local food security, and the more water remains for household and industrial uses. And the more that remains in nature.

That is why the productivity of water use must be dramatically improved. Our Vision relies on meeting about half the increased demand for agricultural water use in 2025 by increasing water productivity, taking many opportunities for improving the management of water. Recycling, widely prevalent, still holds potential for saving water. Gains are also possible by providing more reliable supplies to farmers—through precision technology and feedback irrigation systems.

In the green revolution, getting more crop per drop came from introducing shorter-duration and higher-yielding crop varieties.[1] Adding fertilisers and expanding irrigation have also pushed up yields and water productivity.

How can productivity be further improved in agriculture—the largest water user? The same conditions should be introduced as elsewhere: payment for water services, accountability of managers to users, and competition among public and private suppliers. Then there are the technical and management options to improve productivity.

First, through ever better agronomic practices, the traditional focus of agricultural research:

- *Improving crop varieties.* Plant breeding, possibly aided by biotechnology, plays an important role in developing more drought resistant varieties or varieties that yield more mass per unit of water consumed by transpiration.

- *Substituting crops.* Switching to a crop that consumes less water or switching to a crop with higher economic or physical productivity per unit of transpiration.

- *Improving cultural practices.* Better soil management, fertilisation, and pest and weed control increase the productivity of land and often of water consumed.

And second, deserving more attention, through better water management:

- *Improving irrigation water management.* Better timing of water supplies can reduce stress at critical crop growth periods, increasing yields. This requires making irrigation system management responsive to the needs of farmers.

- *Using more deficit, supplemental, and precision irrigation.* With water under better control, it is possible to use more productive on-farm practices. Deficit irrigation is aimed at increasing productivity per unit of water with irrigation strategies that do not meet full evaporative requirements. Having irrigation supplement rainfall can increase the productivity of water when a limited supply is made available to crops at critical periods. Precision irrigation—using water-conservation technology as well as better information and communication technologies—can reduce non-beneficial evaporation, apply water uniformly to crops, and reduce stress.

- *Reallocating water from lower- to higher-value uses.* Shifting from agriculture to municipal and industrial uses—or from low-value to high-value crops—can increase the economic productivity or value of water.

The keys to increasing food production without a major increase in water use will likely be to increase yields in rainfed agriculture and to close the yield gap by increasing yields where they are far below their biological and technical potential. Neither of these strategic directions will be easy or cheap. But limits to the water available for agricultural expansion may well force our hand.

Increasing storage

The other half of increased demand for water for food and rural development will have to be met by developing additional water supplies. It is imperative that we find ways to develop water supplies—that is, store water for later use, with lower economic, social, and environmental costs. Under the World Water Vision an additional 150 cubic kilometres of storage will be required for irrigation by 2025. Another 200 cubic kilometres of storage might be required to replace the current overconsumption of groundwater.

Rather than relying primarily on large dam projects to provide this storage, the demand should be met using a mix of:

- Large and small dams.

- Groundwater recharge.

New techniques and institutional mechanisms are urgently needed to recharge groundwater aquifers, to avoid the disasters looming if current overdraughts continue

- Traditional small-scale water storage techniques and rainwater harvesting.

- Water storage in wetlands.

New techniques and institutional mechanisms are urgently needed to recharge groundwater aquifers, to avoid the disasters looming if current overdraughts continue. Such mechanisms will include limiting access and providing incentives to users to limit or stop overpumping. Rainwater harvesting, generally a socially attractive alternative to large construction, provides opportunities for decentralised, community-based management of water resources.

Changing the way we manage water
New institutional mechanisms are needed for managing water. Among the most vital are:

- *Pricing of water services at full cost.* Making water available at low cost, or for free, does not provide the right incentive to users. Water services need to be priced at full cost for all users, covering all costs related to operation and maintenance for all uses and investment costs for at least domestic and industrial uses. The basic water requirement needs to be affordable to all, however, and pricing water services does not mean that governments give up targeted, transparent subsidies to the poor.

- *Service-oriented management.* The focus has to be on making managers responsive to user needs. This requires a mutual dependency that can take various forms, including service agreements. The service needs and expectations of users will be influenced by the price they have to pay for services, especially when they have to pay the full cost.

- *Empowering communities, women, and men.* People's initiative and capacity for self-reliance need to be put at the centre of planning and action for water supply and sanitation. Doing so can lead to systems that encourage genuine participation by empowered women and men, improving sustainable living conditions for all—particularly women and children.

Increasing cooperation in international basins
Nearly half the world is situated in 250–300 international river basins—rivers that cross national boundaries and whose resources are shared. Experience shows that shared water resources can be a source of cooperation rather than conflict. Most successful cooperation appears to evolve in stages:

- *Confidence building.* Countries that share international rivers usually start with low-level technical cooperation that focuses on exchange of data or jointly gathered data.

- *Cooperation.* As mutual trust and confidence increase, and as issues appear that concern all parties and can be more effectively addressed through collective action, cooperation gradually grows to a point where countries are willing to undertake joint action or allocate more significant resources.

- *International agreements.* After years of successful cooperation, lengthy negotiations are usually required to reach bilateral or regional agreements.

- *International law and alternative dispute resolution.* Once international agreements have been established, conflicts can be addressed through formal mechanisms (the judiciary or international law) or dispute resolution mechanisms (mediation or arbitration).

Valuing ecosystem functions
Much more research is needed to improve our understanding of ecosystem functions and to value the services that these systems provide. Recent global assessments of the services provided by freshwater ecosystems (watersheds, aquifers, and wetlands) for flood control, irrigation, industry, recreation, waterway transportation, and the like come up with estimates of several trillion dollars annually.

Such knowledge will allow careful assessments of the impacts of water resource use and development on ecosystems, particularly tropical ecosystems. That work needs to emphasise the river basin as the appropriate scale of management—from the forests in upper watersheds to coastal zones affected by the inflows of rivers into wetlands, lagoons, and mangrove ecosystems.

Many practices adopted to manage water for human needs—rules on extracting and sharing water, changes in cultivation and irrigation to save water for other purposes, returns to traditional and community-based water harvesting and storage methods—will also benefit ecosystems. Other measures include reducing nutrients through farm-based manure stor-

Much more research is needed to improve our understanding of ecosystem functions and to value the services that these systems provide

age, controlling silt by reducing erosion upstream, planning for joint hydropower generation and dry season irrigation, and reducing pollutants from agriculture and industry. Above all, ecosystems will be protected by integrated land and water resource management, basin by basin—along with full cost pricing for water services and management reforms for water delivery and wastewater disposal.

Supporting innovation

Increasing productivity will depend largely on innovation, through both fundamental research and the widespread dissemination and adoption of its results.

A key to this innovation will be increased awareness of water issues and the education and training of people capable of bringing about the necessary changes. Once water is appropriately valued, users and producers will have incentives to conserve it and to invest in innovation.

While pricing water is expected to be the primary way to bring in the private sector, a host of public goods aspects of water resources will continue to require public funding. Such activites range from researching staple food crops in developing countries to finding cures for tropical diseases—important to populations in markets too small to make privately funded research financially attractive.

Mobilising financial resources

Total investment in water services today—excluding direct investment by industry—is $70–80 billion a year. The largest investor in services is government—the traditional public sector, which contributes about $50 billion a year. The private sector, ranging from small water vendors to private municipal and metropolitan utilities, contributes around $15 billion. International donors contribute a further $9 billion for both water and sanitation services and irrigation and drainage.The international private sector—an investment newcomer—contributes about $4 billion a year.

We estimate that to achieve the World Water Vision, those investments will have to rise to $180 billion (table 2). Private firms—domestic and international—will be the main source of finance, and local communities will contribute much in cash and in kind. Government resources will be a smaller share in direct capital investment and maintenance costs for traditional water supply projects. This will free up public (and softer loan and grant) resources for water-related projects that supply public goods (such as flood management and

Table 2 Annual investment requirements for water resources

To achieve our Vision in 2025, we need to invest $180 billion a year—for a total of $4.5 trillion.

	Billions of U.S. dollars		Share (%)	
Use	1995	Vision 2025	1995	Vision 2025
Agriculture	30–35	30	43–50	17
Environment and industry	10–15	75	13–21	41
Water supply and sanitation	30	75	38–43	42
Total	70–80	180	100	100

Source: World Water Vision staff.

environmental protection) and for subsidies to low-income and disadvantaged women and men to pay the cost of their minimum water and sanitation needs.

This explicit subsidy explains why government cash flows should remain at current levels, making total cash requirements greater than the direct investments in table 2. The role of government is to provide a regulatory and policy framework for investments to ensure financial sustainability.

Donors need to provide strategic assistance in developing policies, regulations, institutional capacity, human resources, and the technical and scientific competencies to manage the resource base and water services in a fully integrated fashion. Donors will also be important in helping countries meet basic needs and protect the environment. It is recommended that donors support integrated management and social and non-commercial uses of water.

Our Vision for water and life in 2025

By 2025 we will have achieved the three primary objectives of integrated water resource management:

● Empowering women, men, and communities to decide on the level of access to safe water and hygienic living conditions and on the types of water-using economic activities that they desire—and to organise to obtain it.

Water services will be planned for sustainability, and good management, transparency, and accountability will be standard

- Producing more food and creating more sustainable livelihoods per unit of water applied (more crops and jobs per drop), and ensuring access for all to food required for healthy and productive lives.

- Managing water use to conserve the quantity and quality of freshwater and terrestrial ecosystems that provide services to humans and all living things.

In our World Water Vision the five key actions to achieve these objectives are to:

- Involve all stakeholders in integrated management.

- Move   vards full-cost pricing of all water services.

- Increase public funding for research and innovation in the public interest.

- Increase cooperation in international water basins.

- Massively increase investments in water.

How, then, will the water world look in 2025? Almost every woman and man, girl and boy in the world's cities, towns, and villages will know the importance of hygiene and enjoy safe and adequate water and sanitation. People at the local level will work closely with governments and nongovernmental organisations, managing water and sanitation systems that meet everybody's basic needs without degrading the environment. People will contribute to these services according to the level of service they want and are willing to pay for. With people everywhere living in clean and healthy environments, communities and governments will benefit from stronger economic development and better health.

Empowering women and men

New management—transparent and accountable. Water services will be planned for sustainability, and good management, transparency, and accountability will be standard. Inexpensive water-efficient equipment will be widely available. Rainwater harvesting will be broadly applied. Municipal water supplies will be supplemented by extensive use of reclaimed urban wastewater for nonpotable uses (and even for potable uses in seriously water-short urban areas). On small islands and in some dry coastal areas, desalination will augment the water supply. Many cities and towns will use low- or no-water sanitation systems, managed by communities and local authorities.

Secure and equitable access to and control of resources—and fair distribution of the costs and associated benefits and opportunities derived from conservation and development—will be the foundation of food and water security. Efforts to overcome sector-oriented approaches and to integrate catchment management strategies will continue to be supported by wider social and institutional changes. At the turn of the 21st century many government institutions will have recognised grassroots community-based initiatives—and built extensively on this groundwork. All new central government policies and legislation will be subject to prior assessment of their impacts on various stakeholders and beneficiaries. Private and public institutions will be more accountable and oriented towards the local delivery of services. They will fully incorporate the value of ecosystem services in their cost-benefit analysis and management.

More power for communities. At local levels the empowerment of women, traditional ethnic groups, and poor and marginalised people will make local communities and weak nations stronger, more peaceful, and more capable of responding to social and environmental needs. Institutional structures, including river basin commissions and catchment committees, will actively support the equitable distribution of goods and services from freshwater ecosystems. Both husbands and wives will be voting members in water user associations in farming communities. Clear property and access rights and entitlements will ensure that individuals and organisations holding those rights meet their associated responsibilities.

Producing more food and using water more productively

Higher crop yields. Extensive field research on water management policies and institutions in developing countries early in the 21st century will have focused on bringing average yields closer to yields achieved by the best farmers. Closing the yield gap makes the rural livelihoods of poor women and men much more sustainable. Countries with a basic policy of food self-sufficiency and the capability to implement it will increase their yields and production. They will do so by increasing the productivity of water through technical and institutional innovation, up to economic and technical limits. China and India will be among them.

Drawing on technological innovations as well as traditional knowledge, large improvements will be made in agriculture. Genetically modified crops will initially have been introduced on a small scale given lack of public and political support. The

Water management in 2025 will be based on recognising the environmental goods and services that healthy catchments provide

biggest advances in food production in the century's first decade will be plant improvements through tissue culture and marker-aided selection, crop diversity (especially indigenous varieties), appropriate cropping techniques, and soil and water conservation. In 2025, as the industry has demonstrated its responsibility and gained credibility, the use of genetically modified crops will become common and greatly increase the crop reliability in drought-prone regions.

More efficient use. There will likely be a 10% increase in water withdrawals and consumption to meet agricultural, industrial, and domestic requirements. Food production will increase 40%, made possible in part because people recognise that water is not only the blue water in rivers and aquifers, but also the green water in soil. Recognition of rainfed agriculture's crucial role in the water cycle will help make it more productive while conserving aquatic and terrestrial ecosystems.

Only a small part of the water delivered to industrial and domestic uses will be consumed by evaporation—most will be returned after treatment to the ecosystems from which it is drawn. Industrial and domestic water reuse will be common, and non–water-based systems of sewage treatment and other methods of ecosanitation will be applied in many areas to reduce pollution and make full use of human waste as fertiliser. Seminatural and artificial wetlands will be used to improve polluted waters and treat domestic effluents. Countries that face water scarcities early in the century will invest in desalination plants—or reduce the water used in agriculture, transfer it to other sectors, and import more food.

Smarter investments. Investments in cleaner technologies and reduced water and wastewater use will continue to help many industries lower their production costs while reducing their effluent taxes. Development investments will be based on economic valuations and linked to compliance with the environmental assessment and management standards of the International Standards Organization 14000 series.

Conserving ecosystems

Less pollution—more recharge. Concerns about polluting groundwater through leaching nitrates and other chemicals will be addressed. Restrictions will be placed on fertilisers, pesticides, and other chemicals in recharge areas after research on maximising the rate of recharge and controlling pollution. Ideally, the recharge areas will not be used for any other purpose. But in densely population areas, land will simply be too valuable to be set aside for this single use.

Healthier catchments. Water management in 2025 will be based on recognising the environmental goods and services that healthy catchments provide. Catchments require constant maintenance, to be provided largely by local communities, for erosion control, water quality, and biodiversity conservation, among other tasks. Strategic or unique natural ecosystems will be highly valued. And conservation programmes will reflect the needs and involvement of the local communities that depend on them.

More innovation. Innovation in most areas of water resource management—supported by the best of science and traditional knowledge—will accelerate. It will also support development and management of freshwater and related ecosystems. Science and modern technologies will provide an analytical perspective to problem-solving. Traditional knowledge, the wealth of many generations of water resource management, will also be a natural part of decisionmaking. The dialogue between scientists and the holders of traditional knowledge will prompt innovation in resource management.

Better governance. Governance systems in 2025 will facilitate transboundary collaborative agreements that conserve freshwater and related ecosystems and maintain local livelihoods. Management and decisionmaking will generally take place at the most effective and efficient level, helping to set up more open dialogue, information exchange, and cooperation. Despite huge efforts, transboundary conflicts will still be the most difficult water resource conflicts to resolve in 2025.

There will still be much to do, but we will have made the progress needed to mitigate the water crisis that reigned in 2000 and to advance to sustainable water use and development.

*   *   *

To conclude: there is a water crisis, but it is a crisis of management. We have threatened our water resources with bad institutions, bad governance, bad incentives, and bad allocations of resources. In all this, we have a choice. We can continue with business as usual, and widen and deepen the crisis tomorrow. Or we can launch a movement to move from Vision to action by making water everybody's business.

Note

1. "More crop per drop" is the motto of the International Water Management Institute in Sri Lanka.

Vision Statement and Key Messages

Our Vision is a world in which all people have access to safe and sufficient water resources to meet their needs, including food, in ways that maintain the integrity of freshwater ecosystems. The Vision exercise's ultimate purpose is to generate global awareness of the water crisis that women and men face and of the possible solutions for addressing it. This awareness will lead to the development of new policies and legislative and institutional frameworks. The world's freshwater resources will be managed in an integrated manner at all levels, from the individual to the international, to serve the interests of humankind and planet earth—effectively, efficiently, and equitably.

Will continuing the way we manage water lead to a crisis? Yes. Indeed, many countries are already suffering a water crisis that affects their people and the ecosystems we all depend on. More than 1 billion people lack access to safe drinking water. More than 3 billion lack access to sanitation. Several countries lack sufficient water to produce food. And with increasing populations and demands on water, other countries will join them. We have already destroyed about half of the world's wetlands.

Even in a world where water resources are well managed and human demands are met, water withdrawals and consumption by and for humans could be 10% higher in 2025 than in 1995. With current practices, the degradation of ecosystems and the loss of biodiversity will threaten the lives of future generations. It is clear that we must change our ways.

To ensure the sustainability of water, we must view it holistically, balancing competing demands on it—domestic, agricultural, industrial (including energy), and environmental. Sustainable management of water resources requires systemic, integrated decisionmaking that recognises the interdependence of three areas. First, decisions on land use also affect water, and decisions on water also affect the environment and land use. Second, decisions on our economic and social future, currently sectoral and fragmented, affect hydrology and the ecosystems in which we live. Third, decisions at the international, national, and local levels are interrelated.

The three primary objectives of integrated water resource management are to:

● Empower women, men, and communities to decide on their level of access to safe water and hygienic living conditions and on the types of water-using economic activities they desire—and to organise to achieve them.

Vision Statement and Key Messages

- **Involve all stakeholders in integrated management**

- **Move to full-cost pricing of water services**

- **Increase public funding for research and innovation**

- **Increase cooperation in international water basins**

- **Massively increase investments in water**

● Produce more food and create more sustainable livelihoods per unit of water applied (more crops and jobs per drop), and ensure access for all to the food required for healthy and productive lives.

● Manage human water use to conserve the quantity and quality of freshwater and terrestrial ecosystems that provide services to humans and all living things.

Actions needed

Five primary actions are needed to achieve these objectives:

● *Involve all stakeholders in integrated management.* The current fragmented framework for water management cannot deal with the interrelationships identified at Dublin and Rio (box 1.1). Today water professionals manage most water, often on a sectoral basis, without coordinating their planning and operations, without close collaboration with the environmental community, and within administrative boundaries that usually ignore the natural surface and groundwater basin divides. Worst of all, the most interested stakeholders—the women and men in the community whose lives and livelihoods depend on wise water management—do not participate in decision-making. These stakeholders must be involved in making social and economic decisions affecting land and water use.

Governments should establish the institutional mechanisms to make this happen—including national legislation requiring land and water planning and management with participation of women and other stakeholders representing the economic, environmental, and social interests of the community and full sharing of information.

● *Move to full-cost pricing of water services for all human uses.* Because of its scarcity, water must be treated as an economic good. To give this concept meaning, this Report recommends that consumers be charged the full cost of providing water services. That is, they should pay the full cost of obtaining the water they use and the full cost of collecting, treating, and disposing of their wastewater. This does not preclude governments from providing targeted, transparent subsidies to the poor, always taking into account the other calls on public funds. It is a paradox that the poor suffer the most from water subsidies and from policies that treat water as a social good. Too often, water subsidies are captured by the wealthy, leaving insufficient resources for system operation and expansion and resulting in rationing—with the poor always at the end of the line. Pricing water services is a good

step towards establishing a framework that will eventually recognise the full economic value of water, including the cost of externalities.

Full-cost pricing must be accompanied by targeted, transparent subsidies to low-income communities and individuals to allow them to pay to meet their minimum requirements and to encourage user participation in decisionmaking. This approach to valuing water will encourage infrastructure investments and private sector involvement and provide the revenue to cover the costs of operation and maintenance. It will make water suppliers accountable to users. It will reduce water withdrawals from and pollution of ecosystems. And it will encourage the use of water-saving practices and technologies, as well as further research.

● *Increase public funding for research and innovation in the public interest.* The consultations that were part of the World Water Vision exercise revealed that because water and the environment have not been valued, there are enormous gaps in our quantitative knowledge about freshwater ecosystems. Similarly, there is little stimulus for innovation in water conservation technologies. Pricing water resources will encourage the private sector to do some of this.

Still more publicly funded research is needed to promote the development and dissemination of innovative technological,

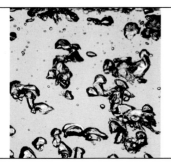

The real revolution in water resource management will come when stakeholders have the power to manage their own resources

social, and institutional approaches to international water resource management, especially in areas serving the public interest and not addressed by market-driven research and development.

● *Recognise the need for cooperation on integrated water resource management in international river basins.* There have been many public cries for cooperative management of international water basins. In general, such cooperation has been driven by other factors that bring the parties together. This probably will continue to be the case. But the Vision goes beyond the usual appeals for cooperation and recommends that nations voluntarily restrict their sovereignty to make it possible to apply the principles of integrated water resource management in international watercourses.

● *Massively increase investments in water.* Addressing the world's water resource problems will require massive investments. More investments are needed in water infrastructure—from current levels of $70–80 billion a year to about $180 billion, with $90 billion coming mainly from the local private sector and communities, including contributions in kind. Coupled with this added investment would be government subsidies targeted to reach the poor (effectively and efficiently) so that they benefit from the new infrastructure. Pricing water to produce the cash flow for future investments and for operation and maintenance should go a long way towards making this possible. Contrary to a lot of thinking today, the Vision recommends that governments maintain their water budgets at current levels, mainly to provide funds indirectly to low-income individuals and communities who otherwise would not have access to water services and to keep food prices affordable for poor people.

Responsibility for implementation

The biggest challenge in water resource management is institutional. Social organisation, government policies, technology choices, and personal consumption all have an impact. But corruption, fragmented institutions, duplicated efforts, misallocated resources, and authoritarian, centralised practices have routinely raised the costs of doing business. Political will must be marshalled to include all stakeholders, especially women, in decisionmaking.

The real revolution in water resource management will come when stakeholders, where possible, have the power to manage their own resources. The task of politicians is to dispel the idea that water is primarily the government's business. They must facil-

itate representative participatory processes so that water can be managed locally to meet the aspirations of many stakeholders.

The pivotal role of women as providers and users of water and as guardians of the living environment needs to be reflected in institutional arrangements for developing and managing water resources. Socially determined roles and relations of women and men—differentiated by age, class, marital status, ethnic group, and religion—determine how water is managed. Participatory processes must be established so that women and men together decide the relative importance of water's economic, social, and environmental functions. Such democratic processes give women better opportunities to benefit equitably from the use of water resources and to take full part in decisionmaking. Moreover, such decisions should be made at the lowest appropriate level. For many issues that will be the community, but for international basins it will be partly international.

Public and private management of water must be improved through greater accountability, transparency, and rule of law. Because of social concerns, in many countries the supply of water services has been entrusted to public agencies, which in most developing countries (and many developed ones) have become inefficient, unregulated, and unaccountable. The private sector changes this dynamic fundamentally, because a private monopolist needs to operate under a defined contract (that is, it needs to be regulated).

Once regulation and accountability are established for private companies, it logically follows to do three things: compare their performance with that of public companies, make public companies also responsible to users, and regulate public companies. This process can start a virtuous circle of competition, with, arguably, the greatest benefit being that public companies become regulated, accountable, and efficient. There is clear evidence in the urban water sector that under such circumstances performance improves immeasurably, but the process has yet to start in irrigation.

Water management in each country affects the global social structure, economy, and environment. International institutions have a major role to play in setting standards and monitoring performance within countries against these standards. But inefficiencies beleaguer the international systems. Reform of international institutions in the water sector should provide for greater participation by all stakeholders—not just governments but also the private sector, nongovernmental organisations (NGOs), community-based organisations representing civil society, and consumers.

2.

The Use of
Water Today

Today's water crisis is widespread, and continuing with current policies for managing water will only widen and deepen that crisis

During the 20th century the world population tripled—while water use for human purposes multiplied sixfold! The most obvious uses of water for people are drinking, cooking, bathing, cleaning, and—for some—watering family food plots. This domestic water use, though crucial, is only a small part of the total. Worldwide, industry uses about twice as much water as households, mostly for cooling in the production of electricity. Far more water is needed to produce food and fibre (cereals, fruits, meat, cotton) and maintain the natural environment.

Providing six times more water now than a hundred years ago, an enormous task, has significant impacts on people and the environment. On the positive side:

● A major investment drive, the International Drinking Water Supply and Sanitation Decade (1981–90) and its follow-up—led by national governments and supported through international organisations—ended with safe and affordable drinking water for 80% of the exploding world population and sanitation facilities for 50%.

● Major investments in wastewater treatment over the past 30 years have halted the decline in—or actually improved—the quality of surface water in many developed countries.

● Food production in developing countries has kept pace with population growth, with both more than doubling in the past 40 years. A successful international research program in agriculture—funded through the Consultative Group for International Agricultural Research—has produced higher-yielding varieties, and there has been a worldwide drive to intensify agriculture through fertiliser application and irrigation. A major factor in this success story—in agricultural productivity and farmer-controlled investment—has been the rapid growth of groundwater-irrigated agriculture in the past 20 years.

● In perhaps the biggest achievement of the century, rising living standards, better education, and other social and economic improvements have finally slowed population growth.

The Use of Water Today

- **Today's water crisis is widespread**

- **Green water—and blue**

- **Passing the threshold of what's usable**

But at the same time:

- An unacceptably large portion of the world population—one person in five—does not have access to safe and affordable drinking water, and half the world's people do not have access to sanitation. Each year at least 3–4 million people die of waterborne diseases, including more than 2 million children who die of diarrhoea, according to World Health Organization statistics (WHO 1996). Other sources provide even higher estimates.

- More than 800 million people, 15% of the world population, get fewer than 2,000 calories a day. Chronically undernourished, they live a life of permanent or intermittent hunger (Conway 1999b). Most are women and young children from extremely poor families. More than 180 million children under 5 are severely underweight—more than two standard deviations below the standard weight for their age. Seventeen million children under 5 die each year, with malnourishment contributing to at least a third of these deaths (Conway 1999a). Lack of proteins, vitamins, minerals, and other micronutrients in the diet is also widespread, particularly among children and women of childbearing age (UNICEF 1998).

- Much economic progress has come at the cost of severe impacts on natural ecosystems in most developed and transition economies. The world's wetlands were halved in the 20th century, causing a major loss of biodiversity. Rapidly declining surface and groundwater quality in almost all major urban centres in the developing world threatens human health and natural values. Because of the adverse social and environmental impacts, large dams have become controversial and have lost public support in many places.

- Water services—irrigation water, domestic and industrial water supply, wastewater treatment—are heavily subsidised by most governments. This is done for all the right reasons (providing water, food, jobs), but with perverse consequences. Users do not value water—and so waste it. To a large extent the subsidies do not end up with the poor but are captured by the rich. Water conservation technologies do not spread. There are too few investment funds and revenues to maintain water infrastructure and research and training systems. As a result the sector is conservative and stagnant, not dynamic with a stimulating flow of innovative thinking.

- Unregulated access to groundwater, affordable small electric and diesel pumps, and subsidised electricity and diesel oil have led to overpumping of groundwater for irrigation and to rapidly falling groundwater tables in key aquifers.

- In most countries water continues to be managed sector by sector by a highly fragmented set of institutions. This approach is not effective for allocating water across purposes. It does not allow for the effective participation of stakeholders. And it is a major obstacle to integrated water resource management.

The conclusion: while much has been achieved, today's water crisis is widespread. Continuing current policies for managing water will only widen and deepen that crisis.

The world's water resources

A key characteristic of the world's freshwater resources is their uneven distribution in time and space. Until recently water resource management focused almost exclusively on redistributing water to when and where people want it for their use. This is a supply-side (engineering) approach. But there are many signs that water is running out—or at least getting a lot less plentiful in more places as populations and per capita water use grow—and damaging ecosystems from which it is withdrawn. So, we need to look at what water is used for and to manage these competing claims in an integrated framework.

Think of freshwater as green or blue. Green water—the rainfall that is stored in the soil and then evaporates or is incorporated in plants and organisms—is the main source of water for natural ecosystems and for rainfed agriculture, which produces 60% of the world's food. Blue water—renewable surface water runoff and groundwater recharge—is the main source for human withdrawals and the traditional focus of water resource management.

The blue water available totals about 40,000 cubic kilometres a year (Shiklomanov 1999).[1] Of this, an estimated 3,800 cubic kilometres, roughly 10%, were withdrawn (diverted or pumped) for human uses in 1995. Of the water withdrawn, about 2,100 cubic kilometres were consumed.[2] The remainder was returned to streams and aquifers, usually with significant reductions in quality.

If we are withdrawing only 10% of renewable water resources, and consuming only 5%, what then is the prob-

*Withdrawals for irrigation are nearly 70% of
the total withdrawn for human uses, those for industry 20%,
and those for municipal use about 10%*

Box 2.1 Renewable water resources

Renewable water resources represent the water entering a country's river and groundwater systems. Not all this water can be used because some falls in a place or time that precludes tapping it even if all economically and technically feasible storage were built. *Usable water resources* represent the water that could be used if all economically and technically feasible storage and diversion structures were built. Usable water resources represent the upper limit to consumptive use even with future development.

The *primary water supply* is the amount of water that can be consumed given the current state of development of the water resource. At any point in time, the primary water supply sets an upper bound to the *consumptive use* of water. It represents the first-time diversions of water. Water diverted to a use that is not consumed either flows to a sink or re-enters the river or humanmade flow network and is recycled. Total deliveries, often reported as *withdrawals*, comprise primary water plus recycled water. Total water deliveries depend on how much water is recycled.

Passing the threshold of what's usable

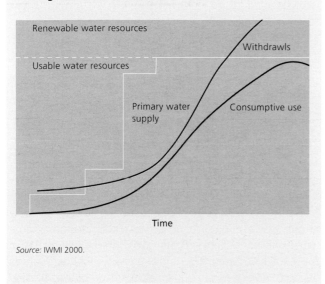

Source: IWMI 2000.

in Asia, and are not available for human use unless stored in aquifers, reservoirs, or tanks (the traditional system in the Indian subcontinent).[3]

● The withdrawal and consumption figures do not show the much larger share of water resources "used" through degradation in quality—that is, polluted and of lower value for downstream functions.

● Water not used by humans generally does not flow to the sea unused. Instead, it is used in myriad ways by aquatic and terrestrial ecosystems—forests, lakes, wetlands, coastal lagoons—and is essential to their well being.

This leads to the following conclusions:

● Even though people use only a small fraction of renewable water resources globally, this fraction is much higher—up to 80–90%—in many arid and semiarid river basins where water is scarce.

● In many tropical river basins a large amount of water is available on average over the year, but its unequal temporal distribution means that it is not usable or that massive infrastructure is required to protect people from it and to store it for later use, with considerable social and environmental impacts.

● In many temperate zone river basins, adequate water resources are relatively evenly distributed over the year, but they are used so intensively that surface and groundwater resources become polluted and good-quality water becomes scarce.

Main uses of water for human purposes

lem? Not all renewable water resources are usable (box 2.1). The numbers may suggest that we are using only a small fraction of the available resources and that we should be able to increase this share fairly easily. Not so, for the following reasons:

● Of global water resources, a large fraction is available where human demands are small, such as in the Amazon basin, Canada, and Alaska.

● Rainfall and river runoffs occur in large amounts during very short periods, such as during the monsoon periods

Withdrawals for irrigation are nearly 70% of the total withdrawn for human uses—2,500 of 3,800 cubic kilometres (table 2.1). Withdrawals for industry are about 20%, and those for municipal use are about 10%.

Water for food and rural development

A key ingredient in the green revolution, irrigation raises agricultural productivity—particularly in Asia, which contains about 70% of the world's irrigated area (figure 2.1).[4] Irrigation consumes a large share of the water it withdraws through evaporation from reservoirs, canals, and soil and through incorporation into and transpiration by crops.

The Use of Water Today

- **For agriculture and rural development**
- **For people and industry**

Table 2.1 Global water use in the 20th century
Although we are withdrawing only 10% of renewable water resources, and consuming only about 5%, there are still problems for human use. Water is unevenly distributed in space and in time—and we are degrading the quality of much more water than we withdraw and consume.

Cubic kilometres

Use	1900	1950	1995
Agriculture			
Withdrawal	500	1,100	2,500
Consumption	300	700	1,750
Industry			
Withdrawal	40	200	750
Consumption	5	20	80
Municipalities			
Withdrawal	20	90	350
Consumption	5	15	50
Reservoirs (evaporation)	0	10	200
Totals			
Withdrawal	600	1,400	3,800
Consumption	300	750	2,100

Note: All numbers are rounded.
Source: Shiklomanov 1999.

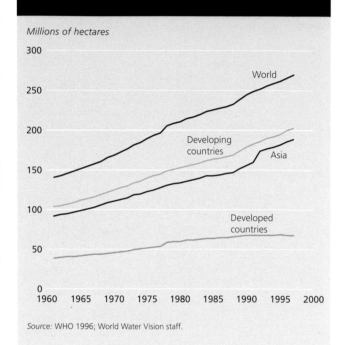

Figure 2.1 Net irrigated area, 1961–97
Irrigated area nearly doubled in the last four decades of the 20th century, mostly in Asia (China, India, Pakistan) and the United States, with the pace of development slowing after 1980 in the developed world.

Source: WHO 1996; World Water Vision staff.

Depending on the technology, consumption can range from 30–40% for flood irrigation to 90% for drip irrigation. The rest recharges groundwater or contributes to drainage or return flows. This water can be—and often is—reused, but it has higher salt concentrations and is often contaminated with nutrients, sediments, and chemical contaminants (pesticides, herbicides) that can damage the ecosystem.

Unless carefully managed, irrigated areas risk becoming waterlogged and building up salt concentrations that could eventually make the soil infertile. This process probably caused the downfall of ancient irrigation-based societies and threatens the enormous areas brought under irrigation in recent decades. By the late 1980s an estimated 50 million hectares of the world's irrigated areas, or more than 20%, had suffered a buildup of salts in the soil.

Perhaps the biggest revolution in water resource management has been the small, cheap diesel or electric pump that gives farmers the means to invest in self-managed groundwater irrigation. In irrigated areas of Pakistan private investment in groundwater development through tubewells (360,000 in 1993 alone) has been an engine of growth. In

India almost half of all irrigated areas depend fully or partly on groundwater. In China more than 2 million pumps irrigate some 9 million hectares (Postel 1999). In the United States one of the world's largest groundwater aquifers, the Ogallala, has been developed through privately financed wells feeding sprinkler systems. While groundwater irrigation has contributed substantially to the world's food production and provided farmers with a dependable source of water, it has also led to massive overuse and falling groundwater tables. A lack of regulation of this common resource, combined with subsidised diesel fuel or electricity for the pumps, gives farmers an incentive to use groundwater as if there were no tomorrow.

Water for people and industry

A large share of the water withdrawn by households, services, and industry—up to 90% in areas where total use is high—is returned as wastewater, but often in such a degraded state that major cleanups are required before it can be reused. The

Cheap pumping and a lack of regulation give farmers an incentive to use groundwater as if there were no tomorrow

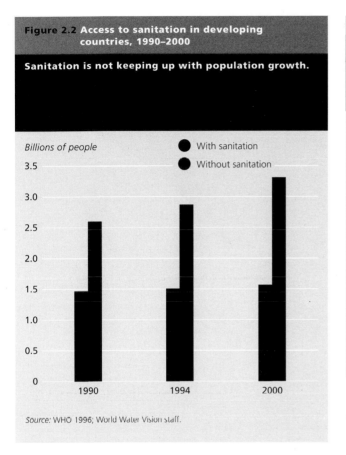

Figure 2.2 Access to sanitation in developing countries, 1990–2000

Sanitation is not keeping up with population growth.

Billions of people

● With sanitation
● Without sanitation

Source: WHO 1996; World Water Vision staff.

Table 2.2 Water-related diseases and deaths

Many children die of easily preventable diseases, and a huge number of older people get sick.

Disease	Annual illness and deaths
Fecal-oral infections (waterborne and water-washed)	
Diarrhoea	1.5 billion cases for children under 5, 3.3 million deaths (5 million deaths all ages)
Cholera	500,000 cases, 20,000 deaths
Typhoid fever	500,000 cases, 25,000 deaths
Ascariasis (roundworm)	1.3 billion infected, 59 million clinical cases, 10,000 deaths
Water-washed infections (poor hygiene)	
Trachoma	146 million cases, 6 million people blind
Infections related to defective sanitation	
Hookworm	700 million infected

Source: Van der Hoek, Konradsen, and Jehangir 1999.

amounts for personal use (drinking, cooking, bathing) are relatively small compared with other uses. And in developed countries the water fit to drink is mostly used to flush toilets, water lawns, and wash dishes, clothes, and cars.

The high per capita residential use rates in North America (around 400 litres per person a day) and Europe (about 200 litres) have declined somewhat in recent years, in response to higher prices and environmental awareness. But in many Sub-Saharan countries the average per capita use rates are undesirably low (10–20 litres per person a day) and need to be increased. In many larger cities of Asia and Latin America the total water produced by utilities is very high, from 200–600 litres per person a day, but up to 70% is lost to leaks. Service is often undependable, and water quality is often unreliable.

The real problem of drinking water and sanitation in developing countries is that too many people lack access to safe and affordable water supplies and sanitation (figure 2.2). The

World Health Organization's *World Health Report 1999* estimates that water-related diseases caused 3.4 million deaths in 1998, more than half of them children. Other estimates are even higher, particularly for diarrhoea (table 2.2).

Behind those grim numbers is a mix of good news and bad. The good news is mainly about water. More people have gained access to safe drinking water since 1980 than ever before. Many countries doubled their provision during that time. And worldwide the provision of new water services is outpacing population growth.

The bad news is mainly about sanitation.[5] Fewer people have adequate sanitation than safe water, and the global provision of sanitation is not keeping up with population growth. Between 1990 and 2000 the number of people without adequate sanitation rose from 2.6 billion to 3.3 billion. Sanitation statistics are less reliable than those for water, however, because some countries have changed their definitions of adequate sanitation.

Inadequate collection, treatment, and disposal of household and industrial wastewater is not just a health hazard for

The water cycle

Blue water, or renewable water resources—the portion of rainfall that enters into streams and recharges groundwater, and the traditional focus of water resource management

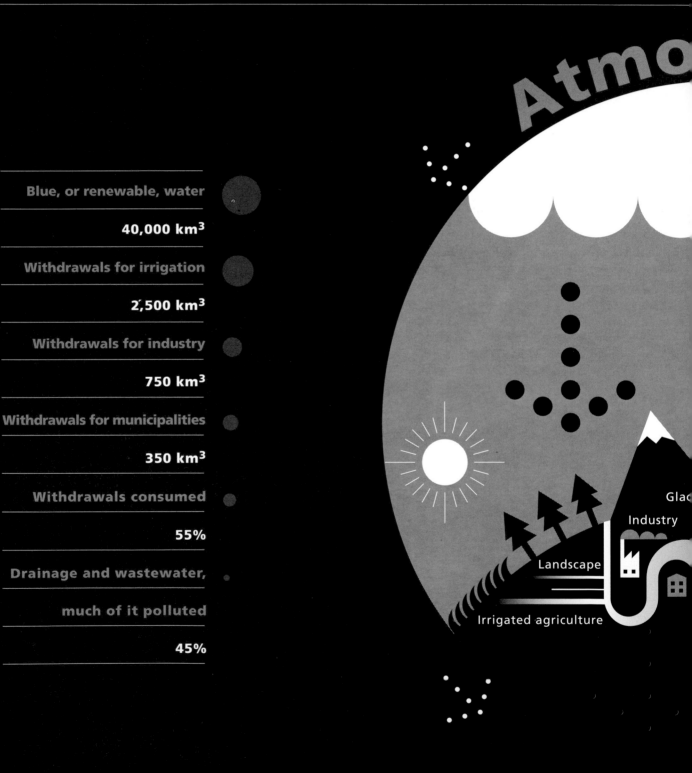

Blue, or renewable, water	
40,000 km³	
Withdrawals for irrigation	
2,500 km³	
Withdrawals for industry	
750 km³	
Withdrawals for municipalities	
350 km³	
Withdrawals consumed	
55%	
Drainage and wastewater, much of it polluted	
45%	

Atmo

Glac
Industry

Landscape

Irrigated agriculture

Green water, *or soil water—the portion of rainfall that is stored in the soil and then evaporates or is incorporated in plants and organisms*

phere

Green water

- Green, or soil, water

  60,000 km³

- Source for rainfed agriculture

  60% of food production

- Primary source for

  terrestrial ecosystems

d agriculture

People

Blue water, blue world

1 **Dynamics of water withdrawal and water consumption**

Irrigated agriculture is the main user of water, then industry, then municipalities.

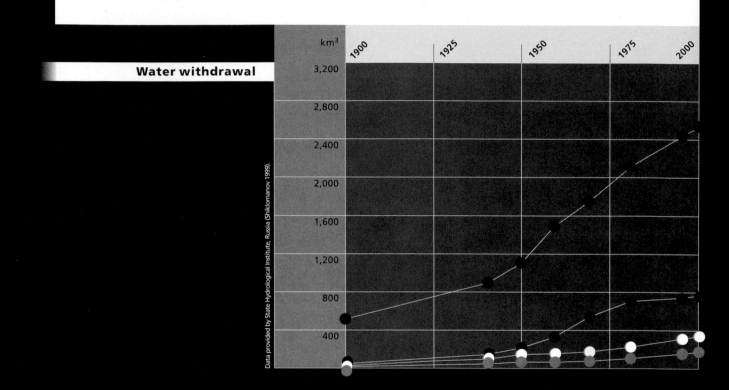

Water withdrawal

Water consumption

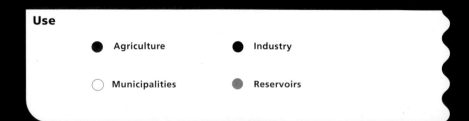

Use

- Agriculture
- Industry
- Municipalities
- Reservoirs

2 | Annual renewable water resources by region

Much renewable water is concentrated in North America (especially Canada), Southeast Asia, and the eastern part of South America.

Annual water resources, km³

	Region	0	1,000	2,000	3,000	4,000	5,000	6,000	7,000
Europe	1. North								
	2. Central								
	3. South								
	4. N. transition econ.								
	5. S. transition econ.								
North America	6. North								
	7. Central								
	8. South								
Africa	9. North								
	10. South								
	11. East								
	12. West								
	13. Central								
Asia	14. N. China, Mongolia								
	15. South								
	16. West								
	17. Southeast								
	18. Middle								
	19. Siberia, Far East of Russia								
	20. Caucasus								
South America	21. North								
	22. East								
	23. West								
	24. South-Central								
Australia and Oceania	25. Australia								
	26. Oceania								

Locations

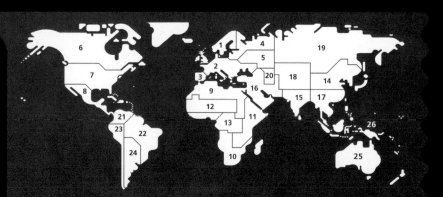

Source of water

● Local resources

● Inflows

The Use of Water Today

humans, it also pollutes aquatic ecosystems—sometimes with disastrous results. Why?

● There is a lingering preference for costly waterborne solutions.

● Supply-driven approaches with high subsidies still prevail in government programmes.

● Promotion strategies are still driven by the suppliers' philosophy of sanitation for longer-term public health benefits, while consumers are interested in better sanitation for more immediate benefits such as status, convenience, higher property values, and privacy and safety.

● The cost of removing 100% of pollutants is prohibitive, so some fraction accumulates in water and soil.

Yet there is good news on sanitation. Large numbers of women and men got better sanitation in the 1990s. New designs and low-cost technologies have significantly expanded the options available to periurban and rural communities.

Many piped water systems, however, do not meet water quality criteria, leading more people to rely on bottled water bought in markets for personal use (as in major cities in Colombia, India, Mexico, Thailand, Venezuela, and Yemen). Bottled water varies from luxury products such as carbonated mineral water in half-litre plastic bottles to filtered groundwater sold in 20-litre containers, and the industry is booming.

Consumption of bottled water in Mexico is estimated at more than 15 billion litres a year, almost doubling between 1992 and 1998, and growing by 35% in 1996 and 1997 alone. In the United States the bottled water market is worth about $4 billion a year, and in the Pacific Northwest the dollar turnover of this "other" water sector rivals that of piped water. A large share of the unserved urban population in many developing country cities has to rely on water vendors who supply water by truck—water of unreliable quality that costs 10–20 times more than piped water (box 2.2). This market for high-priced water bought by low income people demonstrates the failure—or at least the poor performance—of the subsidised, unaccountable, publicly owned water supply model.

Industry consumes just over 10% of the water it withdraws, heavily polluting the fraction that it returns. Industry is a major

---

> **Box 2.2 It's expensive to be poor**
>
> In Port-au-Prince, Haiti, a comprehensive survey showed that households connected to the water system typically paid around $1.00 per cubic meter, while unconnected customers forced to purchase water from mobile vendors paid from $5.50 to a staggering $16.50 per cubic meter.
>
> Urban residents in the United States typically pay $0.40–0.80 per cubic meter for municipal water of excellent quality. Residents of Jakarta, Indonesia, purchase water for $0.09–0.50 per cubic meter from the municipal water company, $1.80 from tanker trucks, and $1.50–2.50 from private vendors—as much as 50 times more than residents connected to the city system.
>
> In Lima, Peru, poor families on the edge of the city pay vendors roughly $3.00 per cubic meter, 20 times the price for families connected to the city system.
>
> *Source:* WSSCC 1999.

---

user in OECD countries and even more so in transition economies, where water use per unit of output is often two to three times higher than in OECD countries and industry can rival agriculture in water withdrawals.

With total annual generation of 2.6 terawatt-hours, hydropower accounts for 20% of electricity production and 7% of energy production worldwide (IHA 1999). In the developed world roughly 70% of hydropower potential has already been developed—in the developing world, only about 10%. In some countries hydropower is the largest source of electricity production. While the construction of dams for hydropower has levelled off globally, several countries have new projects under way.

The power industry returns a large share of the water withdrawn after it has been used to turn turbines in hydroelectric plants or as cooling water in nuclear and other thermal power plants. Industrial water use responds strongly to the price or scarcity of water. As industrial process water gets more expensive, close to 100% of it can be recycled. In the food industry water is an essential production input, but the quantities are relatively small. Water used for cooling in the power industry can be recycled or replaced by other technological options (such as dry cooling towers). Good progress has been made on the treatment of industrial wastewater in OECD countries through enforcement of environmental standards and regulations. Left unregulated, however, and provided with free or almost free water resources, industry is likely to

Rapidly growing cities, burgeoning industries, and rapidly rising use of chemicals in agriculture have undermined the quality of many rivers, lakes, and aquifers

---

Box 2.3 Snapshots of the world's freshwaters and their biodiversity

● Globally, 20% of freshwater fish are vulnerable, endangered, or extinct.

● The rich endemic ichthyofauna of Lake Victoria in Africa have been reduced by predatory Nile perch, overfishing, and eutrophication.

● The Thames River, polluted for centuries, is again habitable by fish.

● Groundwaters as deep as 2.8 kilometres may have rich bacterial flora.

● Agricultural embankment construction in Bangladeshi floodplains, one of the world's largest deltas, threatens the aquatic environment and fisheries critical to the survival of some of the world's poorest people.

● Construction of dams planned for the Mekong River basin threatens fish adapted to seasonal flooding and unobstructed migratory movements.

● Hydroelectric facilities in Brazil have disrupted migration patterns of economically important species, while the Hidrovia channel project in central South America may threaten wetlands and foster invasions of nonnative biota between drainage basins.

● Zebra mussels are paving shallows of the Great Lakes, displacing native mussels and changing ecosystems.

● The number of prairie ponds in North America has rebounded from less than 2 million in 1989 to about 4 million in 1996. And the duck population rose from less than 8 million to nearly 12 million, mostly due to the North American Waterfowl Management Plan (as well as water availability).

● Of 30,000 rivers in Japan, only 2 are not dammed or modified.

● The Ganges and Bramaputra Rivers carry more than 3 billion tonnes of soil to the Bay of Bengal each year, spreading it over 3 million square kilometres of seabed.

Source: McAllister, Hamilton, and Harvey 1997.

be a major water user, causing significant health and environmental impacts through wastewater discharge.

In addition to the three big water users—agriculture, industry, and municipalities—water resources provide a range of other services, such as navigation or recreation and tourism. Water transport is experiencing substantial growth on a global scale, even as its importance has diminished in Europe and North America. Population growth and the opening of economies to the world market are leading to increasing inland navigation in Brazil (Tietê-Paranà Master Plan), China (Yangtze), and Venezuela (with 48,000-tonne push-tows on

the Orinoco). Russia (with 50,000 kilometres of high-capacity waterways) will probably be a leader in this expansion.

Threats to nature—and to people

Freshwater ecosystems have been declining—in some parts of the world, for hundreds of years—threatening the economic, social, and environmental security of human society and terrestrial ecosystems.

Ecosystems and biodiversity

Freshwater and terrestrial ecosystems are integral parts of the water cycle. Their protection requires careful management of the entire ecosystem. For freshwater ecosystems, this implies integrated planning and management of all land and water use activities in the basin, from headwater forests to coastal deltas.

Freshwater biodiversity is high relative to the limited portion of the earth's surface covered by freshwater (box 2.3). Freshwater fish, for example, make up 40% of all fish, and freshwater molluscs make up 25% of all molluscs. Freshwater biodiversity tends to be greatest in tropical regions—with a large number of species in northern South America, central Africa, and Southeast Asia. Worldwide the number of freshwater species is estimated to be between 9,000 and 25,000.

The loss of freshwater biodiversity is poorly monitored except for some larger, commercial species (box 2.4). Available data suggest that 20–35% of freshwater fish are vulnerable or endangered, mostly because of habitat alteration. Other factors include pollution, invasive species, and overharvesting.

Surface and groundwater quality

Rapidly growing cities, burgeoning industries, and rapidly rising use of chemicals in agriculture have undermined the quality of many rivers, lakes, and aquifers. The industrial revolution turned the Thames into a stinking, black health hazard as it ran through London in the late 19th century. Major investments in wastewater treatment and cleaner production have gradually restored its recreational and environmental value.

Most large cities in newly industrialising and developing countries have rivers in the same condition as the Thames in the 19th century. They are a health hazard. They threaten downstream irrigation areas. And they destroy ecosystems. Because of inadequate management, water quality is deteriorating at

The Use of Water Today

- **Polluting groundwater**

- **Rivers drying up**

- **Floods and droughts**

Box 2.4 Disappearing species

Biodiversity losses have been only partly detected and measured. Just a few larger organisms are monitored or considered. But more than 100 fresh-water-associated vertebrates (birds, amphibians, fish) became extinct after 1600, 55% of the extinctions for these three classes.

Worldwide, 20% of freshwater fish are vulnerable, endangered, or extinct; 20% of threatened insects have aquatic larval stages; 57% of freshwater dolphins are vulnerable or endangered; and 70% of freshwater otters are vulnerable or endangered. About 75% of freshwater molluscs in the United States are rare or imperilled. With the possible exception of North America and parts of Europe, nearly all inland fisheries show signs of overexploitation. Cichlid fisheries in Lake Victoria have been replaced by Nile perch catches, but many of the endemic cichlids are extinct. Many stocks of salmonids in western North America have been lost.

About half the world's wetlands have been lost. Ecosystem integrity has declined in about 25 million kilometres of rivers following the construction of dams. Water quality in lakes in populated areas has declined, and many lakes and rivers contain exotic species.

The few rivers whose ecosystems have been restored, like the Thames and the Chesapeake Bay basin, show that restoration of freshwater ecosystems is possible.

Freshwater fish species threatened, selected countries

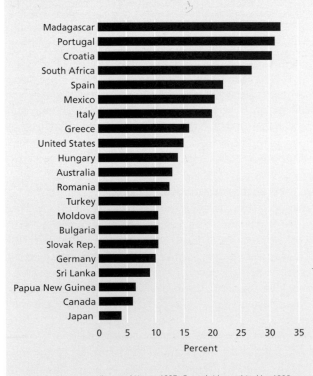

Source: McAllister, Hamilton, and Harvey 1997; Groombridge and Jenkins 1998.

an increasing rate throughout a large part of the world. Much is unknown about the impacts of water resource development on ecosystems, and even basic data on water quality are not available on a global scale. But we can still draw some conclusions:

- There is a critical need to integrate water and environmental management, as provided for under the concept of integrated water resource management.

- Investments are lagging behind urban needs for the collection, treatment, and disposal of municipal and industrial wastewater—and behind rural needs for more efficient irrigation, drainage of surplus irrigation water, and control of agricultural runoff.

- Water quality may be the biggest emerging water problem in the industrial world, with the traces of chemicals and pharmaceuticals not removed by conventional drinking water treatment processes now being recognised as carcinogens and endocrine disrupters.

- Leaks of nuclear waste into aquifers and surface water have not been brought under control, especially in the transition economies of Central and Eastern Europe. A long-term solution for the safe disposal of nuclear waste, to prevent contamination of water resources, has not been implemented anywhere.

- Half the rivers and lakes in Europe and North America are seriously polluted, though their condition has improved in the past 30 years. The situation is worse in developing countries that lack sewerage and industrial waste treatment.

The impacts of agriculture on water quality are less visible but over time as least as dangerous, because many of the fertilisers, pesticides, and herbicides used to boost agricultural productivity slowly accumulate in groundwater aquifers and natural ecosystems. Their impact on health may become clear only decades after their use, but their more immediate impact, through eutrophication, is on ecosystems. These problems accumulate in fresh and saltwater bodies, such as the Baltic and Black Seas.

Groundwater, the preferred source of drinking water for most people in the world, is also being polluted, particularly through industrial activities in urban areas and agricultural chemicals and

Water quality may be the biggest emerging water problem in the industrial world, with traces of chemicals and pharmaceuticals not removed by conventional drinking water treatment processes now recognised as carcinogens and endocrine disrupters

---

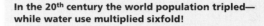
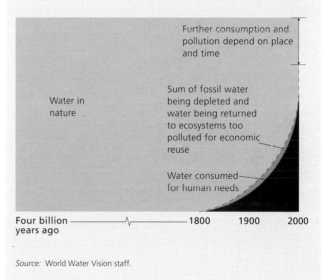
fertilisers in rural areas. In Western Europe so many nutrients are spread over croplands that excess nitrate finds its way into groundwater, ruining drinking water sources in Denmark, France, and the Netherlands. The difficulty and cost of cleaning up groundwater resources, once polluted, make the accumulation of pollutants in aquifers particularly hazardous (box 2.5).

Drying up

Some of the world's largest rivers do not reach the sea. In the wake of economic development of the communities along rivers comes an increase in water consumption that depletes the rivers of their reserves. At the extreme end of the spectrum, the Amu Darya and Syr Darya—two major rivers in Central Asia that feed the Aral Sea—have been deprived of close to their entire water reserves for cotton irrigation. The Huang He (Yellow) River in China did not reach the sea on some days in 1972—or for seven months in 1997. The Colorado River in the southwestern United States and the Indus River, between India and Pakistan, are two of the many other rivers in a similar predicament.

In some countries more water is being consumed by humans than is being renewed by nature (box 2.6). And as populations grow, more countries and regions will be in this unsustainable situation.

Extremes of flood and drought

While the preceding discussion focused on average flows and quality, a key characteristic of water is its extreme events: floods and droughts.[6] Floods sometimes provide benefits in a natural system, and some ecosystems depend on them. Moreover, some people rely on floods for irrigation and fertilisation. But floods are better known for their devastation of human lives and infrastructure (table 2.3).

In the 1990s severe flooding devastated the Mississippi River basin, and thousands of lives were lost to flooding in Bangladesh, China, Guatemala, Honduras, Somalia, South Africa, and most recently Venezuela (White 1999). Internationally, floods pose one of the most widely distributed natural risks to life; other natural hazards such as avalanches, landslides, and earthquakes are more regional (Clarke 1996). Damage, disruption, and deaths from floods are common. Between 1973 and 1997 an average of 66 million people a year suffer flood damage (IFRC 1999). This makes flooding the most damaging of all natural disasters (including earthquakes and drought). The average annual number of flood victims jumped from 19 million to 131 million in 1993–97. In 1998 the death toll from floods hit almost 30,000.

- **Inequalities in use, access, participation**
- **Subsidies**

The economic losses from the great floods of the 1990s are 10 times those of the 1960s in real terms. In addition, the number of disasters has increased by a factor of five. There has been a 37-fold increase in insured losses since the 1960s. Given the trend towards multiple risk insurance cover, which normally includes flood losses, insurance losses will go up even more. Yet the majority without flood insurance will continue to suffer more.

How do floods compare with other natural hazards? They:

- Account for about one-third of natural catastrophes.

- Cause more than half the fatalities.

- Are responsible for one-third of the economic losses.

- Have less than a 10% share in insured losses (figure 2.3).

There are a number of reasons for the increase in the number of catastrophes and in the amount of damage they cause:

- Population trends globally and in exposed regions.

- Increase in exposed values.

- Increase in the vulnerability of structures, goods, and infrastructure.

- Construction in flood-prone areas.

- Failure of flood protection systems.

- Changes in environmental conditions—for example, clearance of trees and other vegetation and infilling of wetlands that reduces flood retention capacities.

Key water management issues

The fragmentation of institutions in the water sector is a serious obstacle to the integrated management of water resources advocated as the desired approach for several decades. The people, organisations, and laws and regulations for water supply and sanitation for residential use often have very little to do with those applicable to the water used for, say, irrigation, flood protection, or hydropower. And surface and groundwater are often managed separately. On top of the fragmented approach within the water sector come the

Table 2.3 Major floods and storms

Floods devastate—people and structures.

Year	Location	Deaths
1421	Holland	100,000
1530	Holland	400,000
1642	China	300,000
1887	Yellow River, China	900,000
1900	Galveston, Texas, U.S.	5,000
1911	Yangtze River, China	100,000
1931	Yangtze River, China	145,000
1935	Yangtze River, China	142,000
1938	Yellow River, China	870,000
1949	Yangtze River, China	5,700
1953	Holland	2,000
1954	Yangtze River, China	30,000
1959	Japan	5,098
1960	Bangladesh	10,000
1963	Vaiont, Italy	1,800
1979	Morvi, India	15,000
1991	Bangladesh	139,000
1991	Philippines	6,000
1991	Huai River, China	2,900
1998	Central America	18,000
1998	Yangtze River, China	3,000
1998	India and Bangladesh	2,425

Source: White 1999.

insufficient links to planning and management of other, closely related, sectors. First and foremost is the link to land use planning. As Falkenmark (1999) notes, a land use decision is also a water decision. Planning and management of land and water resources should be closely linked, or better, completed integrated.

Inequalities in use, access, and participation

The supply-oriented approach to water management that has been the main focus throughout the sector until recently—and still is in many places—assumes that making water available to "society" or "the population" will provide adequate access to everybody. It doesn't.

From the experience that supply-oriented projects and programmes do not automatically reach a major group of intended users has come the call for more participatory approaches. About 10 years of experience with participatory approaches to water management have led to a reconsider-

2

Water provided free of charge does not get used wisely, or conserved and recycled

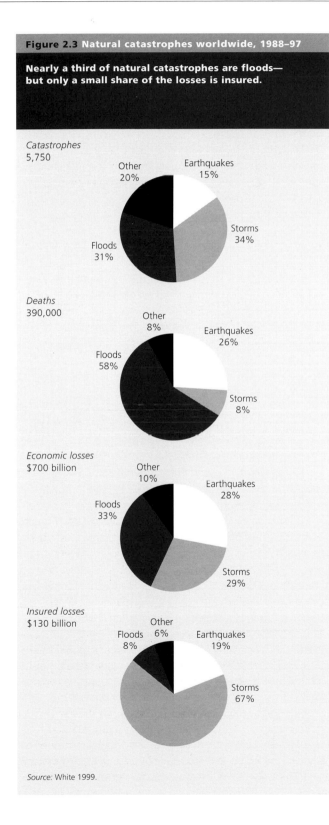

Figure 2.3 Natural catastrophes worldwide, 1988–97

Nearly a third of natural catastrophes are floods—but only a small share of the losses is insured.

Catastrophes
5,750

- Other 20%
- Earthquakes 15%
- Storms 34%
- Floods 31%

Deaths
390,000

- Other 8%
- Earthquakes 26%
- Storms 8%
- Floods 58%

Economic losses
$700 billion

- Other 10%
- Earthquakes 28%
- Storms 29%
- Floods 33%

Insured losses
$130 billion

- Other 6%
- Earthquakes 19%
- Storms 67%
- Floods 8%

Source: White 1999.

ation of technologies and to taking into account the experience, knowledge, needs, and expectations of local water users. Recognition by water agencies of the need to involve and negotiate with different stakeholders—and establish joint management systems—has increased the efficiency and effectiveness of water projects and made water agencies more accountable to users.

At the same time, the experience with participatory approaches shows that identifying who uses water and for what purpose is essential. Communities contain competing interest groups—individuals and groups who command different levels of power, wealth, influence, and ability to express their needs, concerns, and rights. Where water is scarce and vulnerable, those at the lower end of the power spectrum will lose out. Efforts need to be made to ensure that community participation is based on democratic principles that increase social stability and create conditions for all stakeholders to be ensured fair rights, access to information, and an adequate share in decisionmaking.[7]

Most of the 1.3 billion people living in poverty are women and children, the largest groups systematically underrepresented in water resource management (UNDP 1995). The ways water resources are managed in and between different water sectors are highly gender-specific. And a gender-specific division of tasks, means, and responsibilities implies that the different needs, interests, and experiences of women and men need to be taken into account explicitly in water resource management (Van Wijk, de Lange, and Saunders 1998).

Subsidies that mask the high value of water
Governments—or, more accurately, taxpayers—are heavily subsidising irrigation, making both canal water and groundwater available to farmers at no or minimal charge. The direct subsidy to (surface water) irrigation in India, for example, is estimated at $800 million a year, while the indirect subsidy (through subsidised electricity used to pump groundwater) is estimated at $4 billion a year (Bhatia, Rogers, and de Silva 1999).

The fact that water for different uses is often provided for much less than the cost of providing it—or for free—leads users to give it a low value. Water provided free of charge does not get used wisely, or conserved and recycled. It does not give users incentives to conserve water. Nor does it provide sufficient revenues to operate and maintain water systems, to invest in new infrastructure, or to research new technologies. A centralised system that provides low-cost

- **Masking the value of water**
- **Dams and reservoirs**

water but is not accountable or responsive to users can lead to a vicious cycle in which systems deteriorate and require more than normal rehabilitation.

Low water prices have hampered the introduction of water-saving technology and contributed to overuse. It is estimated that 150–200 cubic kilometres more groundwater is pumped each year than is recharged in overexploited aquifers (Postel 1999). As a result groundwater tables are falling by up to several metres a year—with the risk of collapse of agricultural systems based on groundwater irrigation in the north China plain, the U.S. high plains, and some major aquifers in India and Mexico.

Obstacles and options for dams and reservoirs
Of the more than 39,000 large dams (a height exceeding 15 metres) in the 1998 New Dam Register of the International Commission on Large Dams, almost 90% were built since 1950 (Lecornu 1998). They are a large factor in the "irrigation miracle." With a combined capacity of 6,000 cubic kilometres they offer development benefits through hydropower, drinking water supplies, flood control, and recreation opportunities. Dams increase the share of renewable water resources available for human use. But they have also had considerable environmental impacts, and a few very large projects have displaced large numbers of people. In addition to the 39,000 large dams are countless small dams that perform an economic function but block the migratory patterns of fish and reduce naturally nourishing deposits downstream.

Reservoirs are silting up at about 1% a year on average, through soil erosion upstream. Part of this, foreseen in the design stage, has been accounted for in so-called dead storage. In other places developments upstream or incomplete information at the time of design have led to considerable underestimation of the siltation rate, with reduced life expectancies for dams and reservoirs. In any case, some investment is required simply to maintain and gradually replace the infrastructure as it ages. During the 1990s dam construction for large surface water reservoirs slowed to being barely sufficient to maintain current global capacity, let alone expand it at the rates of the 1950s to 1970s.[8]

Dam professionals—such as those in the International Commission on Large Dams and the International Hydropower Association—have undertaken considerable work on possible measures to mitigate dams' impacts. But the general perspective in the environmental community is that mitigation does not work or has not been carried out as foreseen in the feasibility or design phases. Opposition to new large dams has become heated. Because of lack of agreement between dam proponents and opponents on the development effectiveness of dams, respected representatives of both sides agreed to the establishment of the World Commission on Dams, a joint initiative by the World Conservation Union and the World Bank, with private sector sponsorship and significant participation from developing countries. The commission is expected to deliver a balanced analysis of the benefits and costs of dams and the conditions under which their continued development is desirable.

Notes

1. The World Water Vision is based on 1995 data for water availability and use at the national level for residential, industrial, and agricultural purposes; these data are drawn from Shiklomanov (1999). This is essentially the same database, but updated, as used for the United Nations Comprehensive Freshwater Assessment (Shiklomanov 1997) and the International Hydrological Programme's report on world water resources (Shiklomanov 1998).

2. *Consumptive use* is the part of water delivered to a use that evaporates, or is incorporated into products or organisms such that it becomes unavailable to other users. The upper limit to consumptive use within a basin is the primary water supply.

3. In most of India, for example, annual precipitation occurs in just 100 hours. The other 8,660 hours of the year are dry (Agarwal 1999).

4. More than 275 million hectares of land are currently irrigated. An additional 150 million hectares have a drainage system only (Malano and van Hofwegen 1999, based on FAO data).

5. Here *sanitation* refers to the disposal of household wastewater and excreta. However, this waste issue should not be addressed without taking into consideration related community design issues of household solid waste disposal, industrial waste disposal, and drainage.

6. Here flooding is broadly defined as including both excess water caused by rainstorms that subsequently leads rivers to flood (spill over their banks) as well as severe coastal storms or cyclones that can lead to excess water through largely tidal surges.

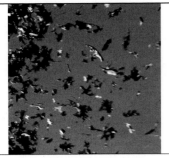

A centralised system that provides low-cost water but is not accountable or responsive to users can lead to a vicious cycle in which systems deteriorate and require more than normal rehabilitation

7. User participation and sustainable solutions may—in the short term, at least—point in opposite directions. The most effective way of preventing groundwater overdraught, for example, is to recognise existing groundwater (property) rights and give the rights holders incentives to limit access and reduce overpumping. Because the existing rights are often not equitably distributed, this leads—at least in the short term—to a conflict between equity and sustainable resource management. We are grateful to John Briscoe for pointing this out.

8. The International Hydropower Association and International Commission on Large Dams estimate that in the 1990s about 300 dams over 15 metres were constructed each year.

3.

3

Water Futures

*Whether the water crisis will deepen and intensify—
or whether key trends can be bent or turned towards sustainable
use and development of water resources—depends on
many interacting trends in a complex system*

Our Vision for water in the 21st century is an expression of a desirable future, based on an exploration of alternative water futures. The alternative possible futures in this chapter form a basis for the Vision expressed in the next chapter. Following a brief explanation of the approach in the Vision exercise (scenarios and models), projected water use and stress in 2025 are explored.[1] Given the wide range of uncertainties affecting the water futures, there is also a wide range in possible uses and stress. This range presents the potential for influencing the outcome through actions focused on key issues that may prove to be turning points.

Turning points in water futures

Whether the water crisis will deepen and intensify—or whether key trends can be bent or turned towards sustainable use and development of water resources—depends on many interacting trends in a complex system. Real solutions require an integrated approach to water resource management. Crucial issues that may provide levers for very different futures include:[2]

Expanding irrigated agriculture
● Will the rate of expansion of irrigated agriculture continue as in recent decades, or will it slow down, as appears to be indicated by reduced investments in the sector?

Increasing water productivity
● Can improvement rates in water use efficiency—or preferably, water productivity[3]—be increased drastically on short notice to ease the water crisis? How can technological and institutional innovation be stimulated to improve these rates?

● Can water productivity for rainfed agriculture be accelerated?

● Will policies emphasise national food self-sufficiency or global food security (involving governance and trade issues)?

Water Futures

Developing biotechnology for agriculture
- What contribution will biotechnology make to increased water productivity?

- Will genetically modified crops gain public acceptance in Europe and developing countries?

Increasing storage
- Can the recharge to aquifers used for irrigation be drastically increased to prevent a groundwater crisis—without major environmental impacts?

- Will there be increasing or decreasing public opposition to large dams in developing countries? Will the hydropower potential in Asia, Africa, and Latin America be developed at the rate of past decades to meet the rapidly increasing demand for electricity?

- How can affordable water storage be created with acceptable environmental and social impacts?

Reforming water resource management institutions
- Will governments implement policies to charge the full cost of water services? Will current trends towards decentralisation and democratisation empower communities to select their own level of water services?

- Will the trend towards transferring management of water systems to water users continue, and will these users be assigned stable water use rights?

- Can governments and the private sector form effective public-private partnerships and develop a service-oriented approach to water management, accountable to users?

- Will countries be prepared to adopt comprehensive approaches to land and water management?

Valuing ecosystem functions
- Will wetlands continue to be claimed for agriculture and urban uses at current rates? Or can this trend be stopped or even reversed? And will wetlands receive enough water of good quality to maintain their biodiversity?

- Will environmental or dry sanitation make the expected breakthrough and become adopted on a wide scale?

- Will there be increased demand for investments in wastewater collection, treatment, and disposal in rapidly developing emerging economies? Will transition economies upgrade their systems?

Increasing cooperation in international basins
- Will countries recognise the need to cooperate as scarcity in international basins increases? Will they make binding agreements on how to share the resources of rivers that cross national boundaries?

Supporting innovation
- Will the public sector increase research funds to foster innovation on public goods aspects of the water sector—such as ecosystem values and functions, food crop biotechnology, and water resource institutions? Can innovation be linked to effective capacity building, education, and awareness raising?

- Will science, with the help of information technology, develop innovative approaches to improve water resource data, real-time methods, seasonal drought forecasting, and longer-term cyclone and flood warnings?

Scenarios and models

Many sector and regional groups explored alternative water futures for the World Water Vision exercise. At the global level three primarily qualitative scenarios prompted the consultations at the sector and regional levels (Gallopin and Rijsberman 1999). These scenarios were the starting point for several model-based simulations of specific components of the water resource management system.[4] The sector and regional visions, the three global scenarios, and the results of the modelling exercises are the basis for the water futures described in this chapter.

The three global scenarios are:

- Business as usual—a continuation of current policies and extrapolation of trends.

- Technology, economics, and private sector—private sector initiatives lead research and development, and globalisation drives economic growth, but the poorest countries are left behind.

- Values and lifestyles—sustainable development, with an emphasis on research and development in the poorest countries.[5]

Between 2000 and 2025 the global average annual per capita availability of renewable water resources is projected to fall from 6,600 cubic metres to 4,800 cubic metres

These three scenarios are not the only possible water futures, and regional and sectoral Vision groups developed scenarios that are equally valid. Many groups and organisations outside the Vision exercise have also developed scenarios of possible or desirable water futures. We are not advocating any of the three global scenarios as the most desirable future. Instead, we explore dimensions of alternative futures. Chapter 4 espouses a Vision.

The approach focused on developing qualitative scenarios to allow incorporation of the many social, economic, environmental, and cultural factors that shape the water future but that cannot be modelled quantitatively. The development and discussion of qualitative scenarios provided a platform for consultation among many stakeholders with different backgrounds and perspectives. Models were then used to analyse the consistency and coherence of the qualitative scenarios, explore some of the consequences, and fill in some of the gaps. The scenarios evolved in four rounds of development, discussion, feedback, and subsequent improvement—with interactions among the scenario developers, modellers, reviewers, and groups working on visions for sectors and regions.

The main forces affecting the global water scenarios are population growth, economic growth, demographic change, technological change, social trends, and environmental quality (Gallopin and Rijsberman 1999). Environmental quality is not a driver in the same sense as the others, because it is also a direct response to them. But it is included here as an important trend to be closely monitored.

Water use is influenced by trends in the drivers, but water use and development is—or can be, when well managed—a driver in its own right, with an important impact on economic growth, social trends, and environmental quality. Recognition of this broad integrated framework is crucial to achieving optimum economic, social, and environmental security through integrated water resource management (annex table 3.1).

The scenarios describe the unfolding of a logical, coherent, and consistent storyline of related trends—but such trends cannot simply be extrapolated. The scenarios show how some trends, following the internal logic of the scenario, would bend or break and how certain actions or policies, if implemented, could influence these and other trends. The scenarios and simulations are not described in detail in this report but in the companion volume (Rijsberman 2000); some of the key results are discussed below.

Projected water use and water stress in 2025

Because of population growth, between 2000 and 2025 the global average annual per capita availability of renewable water resources is projected to fall from 6,600 cubic metres to 4,800 cubic metres.[6] Given the uneven distribution of these resources, however, it is much more informative that some 3 billion women and men will live in countries—wholly or partly arid or semiarid—that have less than 1,700 cubic metres per capita, the quantity below which one suffers from water stress (box 3.1).

WaterGAP model simulations based on the business as usual scenario indicate that by 2025 about 4 billion people—half the world population—will live in countries where more than 40% of renewable resources are withdrawn for human uses. This is another indicator of high water stress under most conditions.

Table 3.1 shows two diverging water use projections for 2025. The projections by Shiklomanov (1999) are based on the assumption that current trends can be extrapolated—that reservoirs will be constructed as in the past and that the world's irrigated area will expand by 30% from 1995 to 2025. The projections by Alcamo and others (1999), with analysis using WaterGAP 2.0 of the World Water Vision's business as usual scenario, assumes limited expansion of irrigated area, which, combined with rapidly increasing water use efficiency, leads to reduced agricultural use but a rapid increase in municipal and industrial use linked to rising income and population (annex table 3.2). The key difference between these two projections—the amount of increase in irrigated land—is the first turning point discussed in more detail later in this chapter.

Even though water use goes up significantly in both projections, neither scenario is based on satisfying the world's water and water-related basic needs, particularly for food production and household use. Alternative futures that satisfy these needs are discussed later in this chapter.

In more developed parts of the world—that is, upper-middle-income and high-income countries—economic growth to 2025 tends to increase water use. But this increase is offset by more efficient water use and the saturation of water demands in industry and households. In addition, the amount of irrigated land stabilises, and water for irrigation is used more efficiently. As a result total water withdrawals decrease.

Water Futures

- **Expanding irrigation?**

- **Or stable irrigation?**

Box 3.1 Assessing the stress on water

Unlike the more traditional concept of *water scarcity*, which focuses on quantity alone, *water stress* denotes reaching the limits of water quantity as well as quality. There is no universally adopted measure of water stress, but perhaps the most widely used is the Falkenmark indicator—renewable water resources per capita a year, often on a national scale. Water stress begins when there is less than 1,700 cubic metres per person a year for all major functions (domestic, industrial, agricultural, and natural ecosystems) and becomes severe when there is less than 1,000 cubic metres per capita. But the Falkenmark indicator does not account for the temporal variability in water availability or for actual use. Its advantage is that the data are widely available.

An indicator that does account for (estimated) use is the *criticality ratio* of withdrawals for human use to renewable resources. This ratio is used for the United Nations Comprehensive Freshwater Assessment and in the WaterGAP model in this Report. The value of the criticality ratio that indicates high water stress is based on expert judgment and experience. It ranges between 20% for basins with highly variable runoff and 60% for temperature zone basins. This report uses a threshold of 40% to indicate "high water stress." The advantage of the indicator is that it is easy to understand and based on water resources as well as use.

The criticality ratio's disadvantage is that withdrawals are not the best estimate of use. Some uses are nonconsumptive and allow reuse, while others consume a smaller or larger part of the water withdrawn. Nor does the ratio take into account available water infrastructure and water management capacity. For example, the ratio shows Belgium and the Netherlands as having very high water stress. This does not mean that these countries face severe water shortages for their projected human uses. Instead, it means that a very large share of their water resources are used—that is, have been developed. In such cases natural ecosystems suffer high water stress because such a large share of the resource is diverted for human use.

A more precise (but much harder to estimate) indicator is the *current basin use factor*. It relates total consumptive use to the primary water supply. When this factor is low—say, 30%—water could be saved and put to more consumptive use. When this factor is around 70% it is difficult and often undesirable to consume more water. Saving water and increasing the consumptive use factor require investment and management.

The *potential basin use factor* relates total consumptive use to the usable water supply. The distinction between the renewable resources in a basin and the primary water supply allows distinctions between physical and economic water scarcity.

- *Physical water scarcity* means that even with the highest feasible efficiency and productivity of water use, countries will not have sufficient water resources to meet their agricultural, domestic, industrial, and environmental needs in 2025. Indeed, many of these countries cannot meet even their present needs. The only options for them are to invest in expensive desalination plants—or to reduce the water used in agriculture, transfer it to other sectors, and import more food.

- *Economic water scarcity* means that countries have sufficient water resources to meet their needs but will have to increase water supplies through additional storage, conveyance, and regulation systems by 25% or more to meet their needs in 2025. These countries face severe financial and capacity problems in meeting their water needs.

Source: Alcamo and others 1999; IWMI 2000.

Table 3.1 Two diverging projections for use of renewable water resources for business as usual

Projections under the business as usual scenario show diverging increases in water use—even without making sure all demands get satisfied—with the largest uncertainty being whether we keep expanding irrigation.

Cubic kilometres

Use	1950	1995	Expanding irrigation 2025[a]	Stable irrigation 2025[b]
Agriculture				
Withdrawal	1,100	2,500	3,200	2,300
Consumption	700	1,750	2,250	1,700
Industry				
Withdrawal	200	750	1,200	900
Consumption	20	80	170	120
Municipalities				
Withdrawal	90	350	600	900
Consumption	15	50	75	100
Reservoirs (evaporation)	10	200	270	200[c]
Total				
Withdrawal	1,400	3,800	5,200	4,300
Consumption	750	2,100	2,800	2,100

Note: All numbers are rounded.
a. Shiklomanov projection.
b. World Water Vision business as usual scenario, Alcamo projections.
c. Alcamo and others do not calculate reservoir evaporation, but since the business as usual scenario developed by the World Water Vision assumes that relatively few additional reservoirs will be built, Shiklomanov's 1995 estimate is used to obtain comparable total use figures.
Source: Shiklomanov 1999; Alcamo and others 1999.

By contrast, higher incomes in developing countries lead to greater household water use per capita, multiplied by the greater number of people. Meanwhile, economic growth expands electricity demand and industrial output, leading to a large increase in water withdrawals for industry. Even though water is used more efficiently in households and industry, pressures to increase water use overwhelm these efficiency improvements.

The result is a large increase in water withdrawals in the domestic and industrial sectors of the developing world, in response to rising population and industrialisation, and higher consumption from higher incomes. In the World Water Vision business as usual scenario analysed by Alcamo and others (1999), the increase in irrigated land does not keep pace with growing food demand. This means that the amount of water

*The rate of expansion of irrigated land
is the most important determinant of water stress,
at least the stress related to quantity*

withdrawn for irrigation decreases slightly (because of efficiency improvements). Even so, agriculture remains the
world's main user of freshwater, making more than half the
total withdrawals. Shiklomanov's projections, assuming
strong increases in irrigation, show a large increase in water
for agriculture. For Shiklomanov's projections to be realised,
dam construction and groundwater extraction will have to
continue apace.

The sum of trends in all sectors: significant net growth in
water withdrawals in developing countries between 1995
and 2025. Adding together the trends in developed and
developing countries under the business as usual scenario
results in an increase in global water withdrawals from 3,800
cubic kilometres in 1995 to 4,300–5,200 cubic kilometres in
2025 (see table 3.1). The difference largely depends on how
much irrigated agriculture does or does not expand.

Because of the increase in water withdrawals, the pressure on
water resources will grow significantly in more than 60% of
the world (Alcamo and others 1999), including large areas of
Africa, Asia, and Latin America. Will this lead to more frequent water crises? That depends on how much water is available relative to withdrawals—and on countries' ability to cope
with increasing pressure on water resources. That is, it
depends on whether countries face physical or economic
water scarcity—and whether they have the resources to overcome economic water scarcity (see box 3.1).

The effect of high water stress will differ in different countries. In developed countries water is often treated before it
is sent to downstream users, and industry recycles its water
supply fairly intensively. For these and other reasons developed countries can intensively use their water resources (as
indicated by a criticality ratio greater than 40%) without
major negative consequences.

Most developing countries, by contrast, do not treat wastewater, and their industries do not intensively recycle their
water supplies. So, the projected intensive use of water here
will lead to the rapid degradation of water quality for downstream users—and to frequent and persistent water
emergencies.

Expanding irrigated agriculture

The rate of expansion of irrigated land is the most important
determinant of water stress, at least the stress related to

quantity. There are two contrasting views on how the trend
in irrigated agriculture expansion will continue or bend, with
important groups of stakeholders weighing in on both sides.

The conventional wisdom in agriculture is that, based on the
need to produce food for the growing world, irrigated agriculture will have to keep pace—and therefore expand by
some 30% in harvested area by 2025. This position, supported by the Food and Agriculture Organization (FAO) and
the International Commission on Irrigation and Drainage
(ICID), is also reflected in Shiklomanov's (1999) projections
and the International Water Management Institute's (IWMI)
first projection (Seckler and others 1998). The conclusion of
these analyses, under optimistic assumptions on yield and
efficiency improvements, is that water use for agriculture will
have to increase at least 17% from 1995.

The other perspective—supported by environmentalists and
by a number of stakeholders in agriculture—holds that a
slowdown in dam building and irrigation investments, combined with the consequences of falling groundwater tables,
will limit the expansion in irrigated area to 5–10%. The consequences of such a scenario were analysed in the Vision's
business as usual scenario (Rosegrant and Ringler 1999;
Alcamo and others 1999; IWMI 2000).

Both scenarios are persuasive. The FAO's longer-term data on
the increase in irrigated area do not show a clear decline other
than in OECD countries. But a slowdown in agricultural investment is a clear indication that the expansion in area is likely
to slow as well. According to Rosegrant and Ringler (1999),
the growth in global irrigated area declined from 2.2% a year
in 1967–82 to 1.5% in 1982–93.

Analysis of the two alternatives shows that neither is
attractive:

● *Unattractive alternative 1.* The 30% increase in irrigated
area requires major investments in water infrastructure, a
considerable part of which would have to be through
large dams. There would also be severe water scarcities
and serious risks of major damage to ecosystems
(Shiklomanov 1999; Seckler and others 1998).

● *Unattractive alternative 2.* A strong reduction in irrigation
expansion—under otherwise unchanged policies, or business as usual as elaborated by the Scenario Development
Panel (Alcamo and others 1999; Rosegrant and Ringler

Water stress

1 | **Water stress in 2025 under the business as usual scenario**

Under the business as usual scenario, by 2025 about 4 billion people—half the world's population—will live in countries with high water stress.

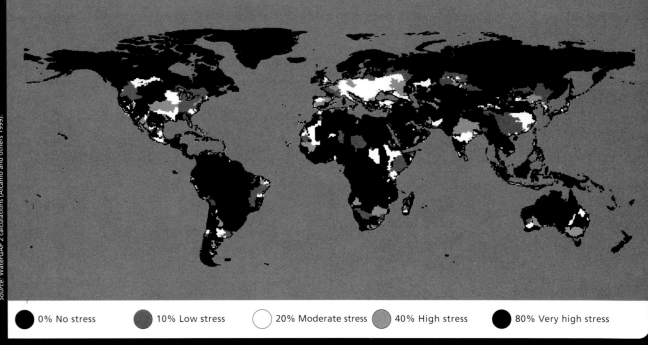

Source: WaterGAP 2 calculations (Alcamo and others 1999).

● 0% No stress   ● 10% Low stress   ○ 20% Moderate stress   ● 40% High stress   ● 80% Very high stress

The ratio of withdrawals for human use to total renewable resources—the criticality ratio—implies that water stress depends on the variability of resources. It ranges from 20% for basins with highly variable runoff to 60% for temperate zone basins. Here we use an overall value of 40% to indicate high water stress.

2 **Change in water stress from 1995 to 2025 under the business as usual scenario**

Many of today's developing countries will experience increasing pressure on water resources.

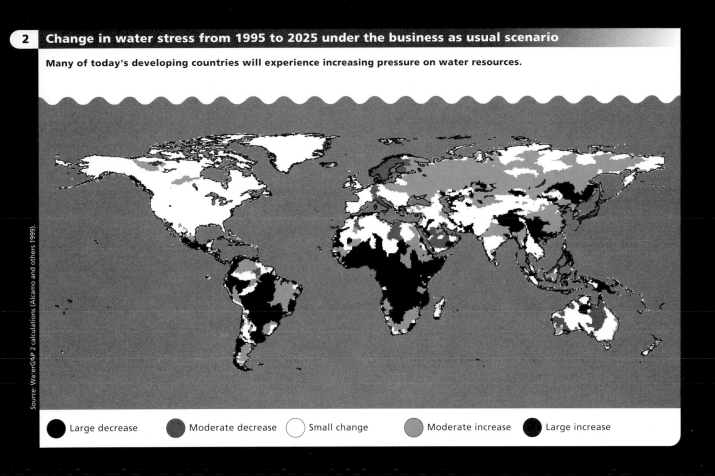

Source: Wa:erGAP 2 calculations (Alcamo and others 1999).

● Large decrease ● Moderate decrease ○ Small change ● Moderate increase ● Large increase

Withdrawals are not the best estimate of use, however. A more precise (but much harder to estimate) indicator is the ratio of consumption to the total actually available. When it is low—say, 30%—more water would be consumed. When it is high—say, 70%—it is difficult and undesirable to consume more.

Water trends

1 Sub-Saharan Africa: Another 175 million people in areas with high water stress

Source: WaterGAP 2 calculations (Alcamo and others 1999).

Under the business as usual scenario, domestic water withdrawals in Sub-Saharan Africa increase from about 10 cubic kilometres in 1995 to 42 cubic kilometres in 2025. Why? Because higher incomes lead to higher per capita water use, even though technology tends to make water use more efficient.

In West Africa in 2025 domestic water use is 34 cubic metres a person—2.1 times its 1995 value but still far below Western Europe's 105 cubic metres a person per year. Industrial water use also increases—from about 3 to 16 cubic kilometres a year between 1995 and 2025.

Because of abundant rainfall, there will likely be enough water to cover the increase in domestic and industrial water use. So, the question is whether water distribution systems can expand fast enough to fulfill the needs of growing population and industry. To cover the growth in water withdrawals, municipal water capacity must expand by 5.5% a year and industrial capacity by 7.1% a year.

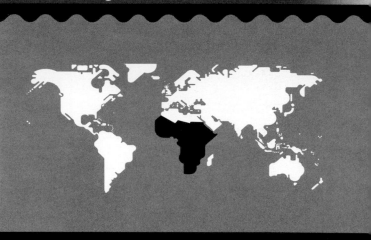

2 Southeast and East Asia: Another 1.3 billion people in areas with high water stress

Source: WaterGAP 2 calculations (Alcamo and others 1999).

In South and East Asia irrigated area under the business as usual scenario grows only slightly between 1995 and 2025, while irrigation efficiency improves. The effect is a decrease in water used for irrigation from 1,359 to 1,266 cubic kilometres a year. At the same time, strong economic growth leads to more material possessions and greater water use by households, increasing water withdrawals for domestic use from 114 to 471 cubic kilometres a year. This economic growth also requires larger quantities of water for Asian industry, increasing from 153 to 263 cubic kilometres a year.

The sum of these trends is an overall increase in water withdrawals between 1995 and 2025. Thus the pressure on water resources will become even greater than was experienced in 1995, when about 6.5 million square kilometres of river basin area were under high water stress. That area increases to 7.9 million square kilometres in 2025. The number of people living in these areas also grows tremendously—from 1.1 billion to 2.4 billion.

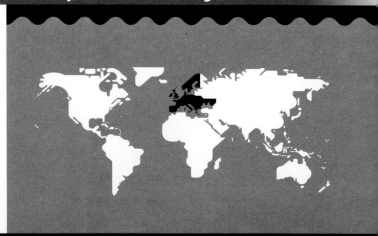

3 Western Europe: Lower withdrawals and higher efficiency, but not much change in water stress

Source: WaterGAP 2 calculations (Alcamo and others 1999).

Water withdrawals in Western Europe are growing slowly or not at all as households, industry, and agriculture become more water efficient. The per capita use of water in households goes up slightly with the economic growth of the business as usual scenario between 1995 and 2025, but the amount of water used by industry per megawatt-hour goes down because of greater recycling and other efficiency improvements. The amount of irrigated area stabilises, and new technology increases the efficiency of irrigation systems so that there is also a decline in the amount of water used per hectare.

Although water withdrawals go down, the pressure on water resources continues to be high in some areas because of the density of population and industrial activity. So, some river basins remain in the high stress category with sharp competition among industrial, domestic, and some agricultural users.

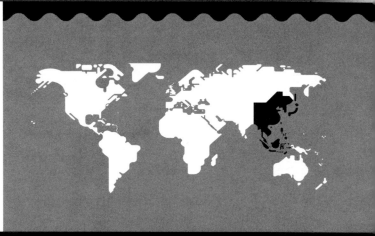

By 2025 half the world's people will live in countries with high water stress

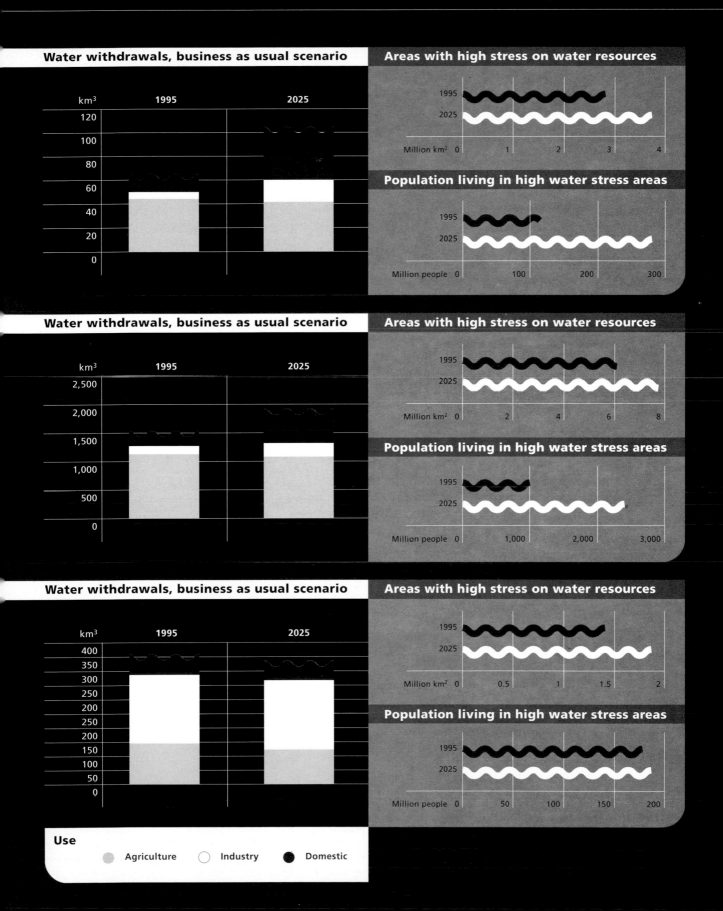

Water withdrawals, business as usual scenario

Areas with high stress on water resources

Population living in high water stress areas

Use

- Agriculture
- Industry
- Domestic

Water Futures

1999; IWMI 2000)—will cause considerable food shortages and rising food prices.

Both alternatives—unattractive and unsustainable—would considerably deepen today's water crisis. Thus there is every motivation to implement policies that make food production and water resource management more sustainable.

Increasing water productivity

At the heart of the question of whether a water crisis can be averted is whether water can be made more productive. The more we produce with the same amount of water, the less the need for infrastructure development, the less the competition for water, the greater the local food security, and the more water for agricultural, household, and industrial uses. And the more that remains in nature.

IWMI (2000) concludes that sustainable water management and food production is possible but requires two major improvements in water resource and irrigation technology and management:

● *Greater water productivity: more crop per drop*. The productivity of water use must be dramatically improved. The IWMI base scenario relies on meeting about half the increased demand for water in 2025 by increasing water productivity, taking many opportunities for improving the management of water. The first task is to understand where these opportunities exist. Recycling, although widely prevalent, still holds potential for saving water. Gains are also possible by providing more reliable supplies—through precision technology and through feedback systems.[7] Supplemental irrigation with low-cost precision technology offers a means for poor farmers to produce more. With competition for water on the rise, these solutions will require major changes in the institutions responsible for managing water.

● *More storage: developing additional resources*. The other half of increased demand must be met by developing additional water supplies, but at much lower economic, social, and environmental costs (IWMI 2000). The additional water storage and conveyance required by 2025 is estimated by the IWMI at some 400 cubic kilometres a year for expansion of irrigated agriculture alone. Such an expansion may be viewed as moderate by the irrigation community, but it is unlikely to be well-received by other users. Feeding

the world without this expansion, however, requires a strategy that puts more emphasis on other ways to increase food production—such as intensifying rainfed production and improving management of water in existing agricultural areas. An additional 200 cubic kilometres might be required to replace the current unsustainable overconsumption of groundwater (Postel 1999). For financial, environmental, and other reasons a large part of the additional storage requirement should be met using a mix of groundwater recharging and aquifer drawdowns, developing alternative methods for storing water in wetlands, harvesting rainwater, and relying on traditional technologies such as tanks and other small-scale alternatives, rather than by building large-scale surface storage facilities alone.

Increasing the productivity of water is central to producing food, to fighting poverty, to reducing competition for water, and to ensuring that there is enough water for nature. Achieving the greater productivity needed to resolve the water crisis will not happen automatically—it will require great effort. But it is possible, especially in developing countries, where water productivity is far below potential. For cereal grains, for example, the range in water productivity—in biomass produced per cubic metre of evapotranspiration—is between 0.2 and 1.5 kilograms per cubic metre. As a rule of thumb, that value should be about 1 kilogram per cubic metre (IWMI 2000). If a country's demand for grains grows by 50% by 2025, one way to match the increase is to increase water productivity by 50%.

Meeting this challenge will require a far greater effort and significant changes in how water is managed. What needs to change? Where are improvements required? The biggest boosts to water productivity have come from better plant varieties and agronomic practices. Getting more crop per drop came from introducing shorter-duration and higher-yielding crop varieties. Adding fertilisers also pushes up yields and water productivity. This was the heart of the green revolution.

With a stable water supply through irrigation, agricultural productivity has risen dramatically in the past 50 years. But scope for improvement remains. In many areas potential productivity is not realised—largely because of poor irrigation water management. Without a stable supply of irrigation water, farmers cannot achieve their production potential.

For example, wheat yields and water productivity vary greatly in three locations with somewhat similar environments (fig-

Increasing the productivity of water is central to producing food, to fighting poverty, to reducing competition for water, and to ensuring that there is enough water for nature

ure 3.1). In a desert environment India's Bhakra irrigation system—across the border from the Pakistani Punjab—supplies a major part of India's breadbasket. The Imperial Valley in California is also in a desert environment. Within the Pakistani Punjab, yields vary greatly—with some farmers as productive as those in California, and some way below the average. Even though production depends on environmental, market, soil, and other conditions not equal across sites, there appears to be scope to manage resources for higher productivity.

In OECD countries industrial water productivity has increased rapidly in the past 20 years, in response to rising prices and stricter environmental standards for industrial wastewater. With the expected increase in the cost of providing water to industry—if users are charged the full-cost price—this trend could accelerate.

How can productivity be improved in agriculture—the largest water user? A precondition is that the same conditions are introduced as elsewhere: payment for water services, accountability of managers to users, and competition among public and private suppliers. Then there are a range of technical and management options to improve productivity. First, through better agronomic practices (IWMI 2000):

- *Crop varietal improvement.* Plant breeding plays an important role in developing varieties that yield more mass per unit of water consumed by transpiration. For example, by shortening the growth period while keeping the same yield, production per unit of evapotranspiration increases. This includes contributions from biotechnology.

- *Crop substitution.* Switching from a more to a less water-consuming crop or switching to a crop with higher economic or physical productivity per unit of transpiration.

- *Improved cultural practices.* Better soil management, fertilisation, and pest and weed control increase the productivity of land and often of water consumed.

And second, through better water management practices:

- *Better water management.* Better timing of water supplies can reduce stress at critical crop growth periods, increasing yields. When the water supply is more reliable, farmers tend to invest more in other agricultural inputs, leading to higher output per unit of water. Controlling

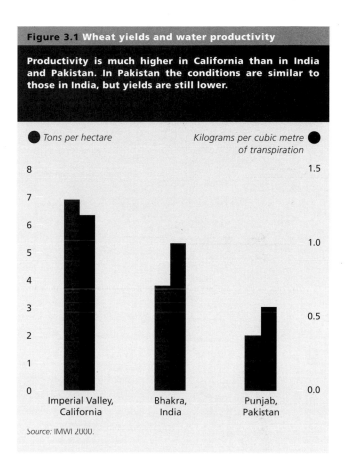

Figure 3.1 Wheat yields and water productivity

Productivity is much higher in California than in India and Pakistan. In Pakistan the conditions are similar to those in India, but yields are still lower.

● *Tons per hectare* — *Kilograms per cubic metre of transpiration* ●

Source: IMWI 2000.

salinity through water management at the project or field level can prevent reductions in water productivity.

- *Deficit, supplemental, and precision irrigation.* With sufficient water control, it is possible to use more productive on-farm practices. Deficit irrigation is aimed at increasing productivity per unit of water with irrigation strategies that do not meet full evaporative requirements. Irrigation supplementing rainfall can increase the productivity of water when a limited supply is made available to crops at critical periods. Precision irrigation, including drip, sprinkler, and level basins, reduces nonbeneficial evaporation, applies water uniformly to crops, and reduces stress, and so can increase water productivity (IWMI 2000).[8]

- *Reallocating water from lower- to higher-value uses.* Shifting from agriculture to municipal and industrial uses—or from low-value to high-value crops—can increase the economic productivity or value of water. As

Water scarcity

1 Business as usual scenario, 2025

Limited investments in new water infrastructure reduce irrigation expansion and prevent water scarcity—but food scarcity is the result.

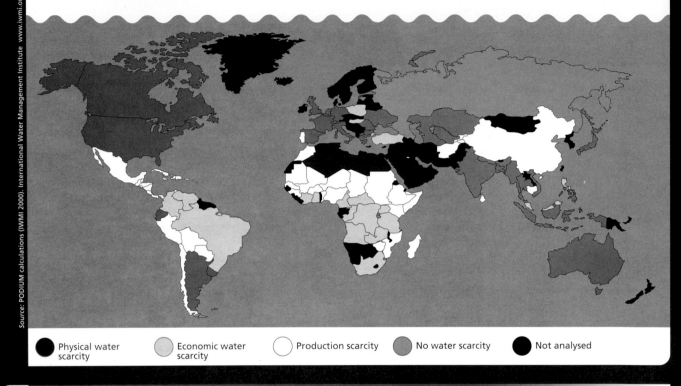

Source: PODIUM calculations (IWMI 2000). International Water Management Institute www.iwmi.org.

- ● Physical water scarcity
- ● Economic water scarcity
- ○ Production scarcity
- ● No water scarcity
- ● Not analysed

2 Technology, economics, and private sector scenario, 2025

Emphasis on technology and investments increases primary water supply by 24%. China and India are water short due to irrigation expansion. Many countries face economic water scarcity.

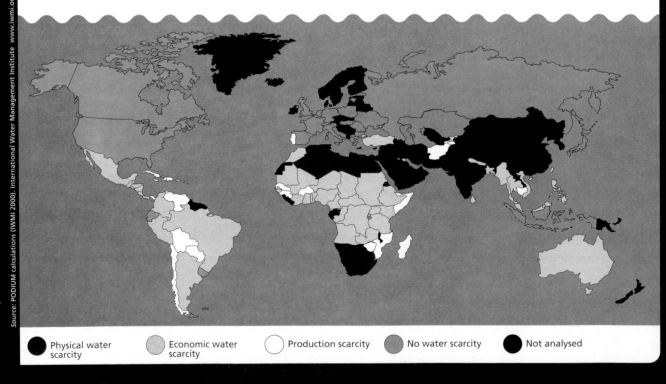

Source: PODIUM calculations (IWMI 2000). International Water Management Institute www.iwmi.org.

- ● Physical water scarcity
- ● Economic water scarcity
- ○ Production scarcity
- ● No water scarcity
- ● Not analysed

A country's ability to cope with increasing pressure on its water resources depends on whether it faces physical or economic water scarcity

3 | **Values and lifestyles scenario, 2025**

Development focuses on low-income countries that face economic water scarcity. Water and food scarcity is limited.

Source: PODIUM calculations (IWMI 2000). International Water Management Institute www.iwmi.org.

● Physical water scarcity   ● Economic water scarcity   ○ Production scarcity   ● No water scarcity   ● Not analysed

● **Business as usual—a continuation of current policies and extrapolation of trends.**

● **Technology, economics, and private sector—private sector initiatives lead research and development, and globalisation drives economic growth, but the poorest countries are left behind.**

● **Values and lifestyles—sustainable development, with an emphasis on research and development in the poorest countries.**

Cereal deficits or surpluses

1 **1995**

Major deficits, mostly in Africa and the Middle East.

Source: PODIUM calculations (IWMI 2000). International Water Management Institute www.iwmi.org.

● Major deficit ● Minor deficit ○ Self-sufficient ○ Minor surplus ● Major surplus ● Not analysed

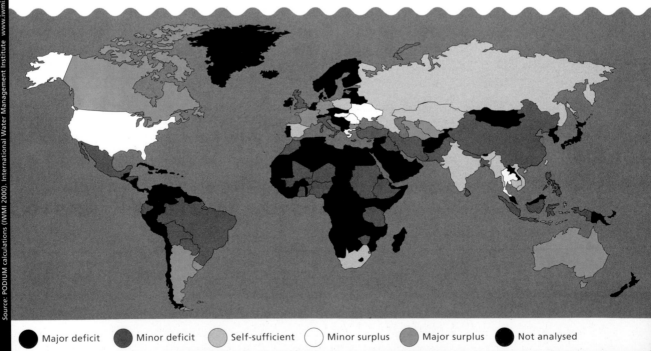

2 **Business as usual scenario, 2025**

Global deficit of 200 million tons—major deficits in many countries in Africa and the Middle East—India self-sufficient.

Source: PODIUM calculations (IWMI 2000). International Water Management Institute www.iwmi.org.

● Major deficit ● Minor deficit ○ Self-sufficient ○ Minor surplus ● Major surplus ● Not analysed

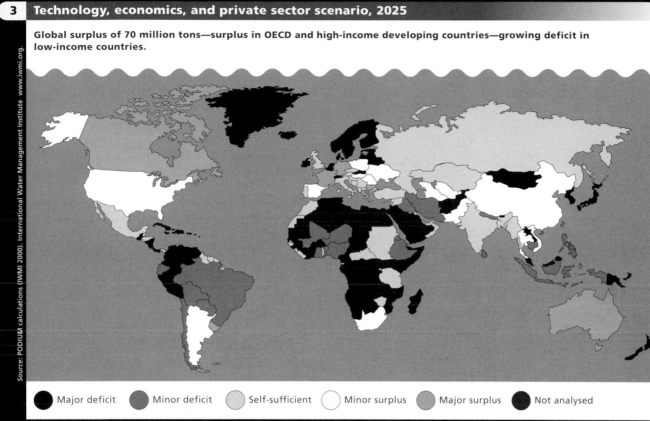

3 Technology, economics, and private sector scenario, 2025

Global surplus of 70 million tons—surplus in OECD and high-income developing countries—growing deficit in low-income countries.

Source: PODIUM calculations (IWMI 2000). International Water Management Institute www.iwmi.org.

⬤ Major deficit　⬤ Minor deficit　⬤ Self-sufficient　◯ Minor surplus　⬤ Major surplus　⬤ Not analysed

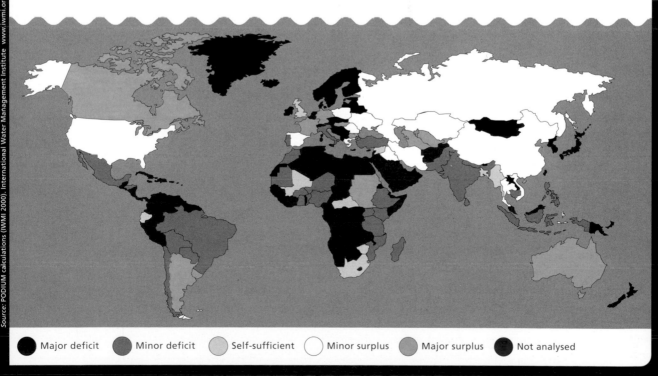

4 Values and lifestyles scenario, 2025

Closing yield gap, rising productivity in low-income countries, lower population growth, and more concern about the environment—deficit in low-income countries reduced.

Source: PODIUM calculations (IWMI 2000). International Water Management Institute www.iwmi.org.

⬤ Major deficit　⬤ Minor deficit　⬤ Self-sufficient　◯ Minor surplus　⬤ Major surplus　⬤ Not analysed

- **The doubly green revolution**

- **Adding more storage**

a result of such reallocation, downstream commitments may change, with serious legal, equity, and other social considerations that must be addressed. One option here is trade in virtual water.

Trade can help alleviate water scarcity (Allan and Court 1996). Countries with plentiful water should export water-intensive crops, such as rice, to water-scarce countries. According to an earlier analysis by the International Food Policy Research Institute (IFPRI) that did not take water into account as a constraint, world trade in food will increase substantially between 1995 and 2020 (Rosegrant, Agcaoili-Sombilla, and Perez 1995). Trade in meat will triple, that in soybeans will double, and that in grains will rise by two-thirds. Developing countries will substantially increase their imports, while the exports will come mainly from the United States, Canada, Australia, and Argentina. The analysis concluded that this increase would satisfy world food demand, but not substantially reduce the number of undernourished people.

More food exports from industrial countries are not a solution for the 650 million poor and undernourished people in rural areas. Most live where agricultural potential is low and natural resources are poor (Leonard 1989). They also live in areas that suffer from periodic or chronic shortages of water. For them, access to water means local production of food that generates employment and income—and is sufficient and dependable enough to meet local needs throughout the year, including years unfavourable for agriculture (Conway 1999a).

A recent IFPRI analysis of the three World Water Vision scenarios also concluded that international trade in food will rise rapidly—for different reasons (Rosegrant and Ringler 1999). If agriculture does not expand rapidly, then the increased trade will largely come from water-constrained limits on food production. Under the other two scenarios—which explore a range of measures to increase food production in projected deficit areas—the increased trade can only be caused by faster economic growth in the developing world, which will lead to additional food demand, outstripping even the local increases in production.

David Seckler has pointed out that the increase in trade will likely be constrained by the need for foreign exchange to pay for the imports (IWMI 2000). Because of strong competition, it is unrealistic to expect all countries to move their scarce resources into the production of higher-value crops. Thus the IWMI scenario assumes that trade will remain at the current

percentage of food consumption—that is, a maximum 30–40% increase in volumes traded (IWMI 2000).

Developing biotechnology for agriculture

According to Conway (1999a), the application of advances in biotechnology—including genetic engineering, tissue culture, and marker-aided selection (which uses DNA technology to detect the transmission of a desired gene to a seedling arising from a cross; box 3.2)—will be essential for:

● Raising yield ceilings.

● Reducing excessive pesticide use.

● Increasing the nutrient value of basic foods.

● Providing farmers on less favoured lands with varieties better able to tolerate drought, salinity, and lack of soil nutrients.

Indeed, biotechnology should be seen as an element of what Conway (1999b) has dubbed the "the doubly green revolution". That revolution consists of ecological approaches to sustainable agriculture, greater participation by farmers in analysis, design, and research, and the application of modern biotechnology to the needs of the poor in developing countries, particularly those in drought-prone areas.

The experts disagree on the potential of biotechnology to increase food production. Seckler, for instance, does not expect biotechnology to add more than 5–10% to the world's food production over the next 25 years (IWMI 2000). Conway (1999a), however, believes that over the next 10 years we are likely to see much greater progress in multiple gene introductions that focus on output traits or on hard to achieve input characteristics, and that a high priority will be to engineer crops for drought tolerance.

He concludes that while the potential benefits of biotechnology are considerable, they are unlikely to be realised without taking some crucial steps. Poor rural farmers in drought-prone regions are unlikely to adopt these crops unless the seeds are provided for free or at nominal cost. This will require heavy public investment, by governments and donors, in the research and distribution of seeds and technical advice. And these efforts will need to focus on crops—cassava, upland rice, African maize, sorghum, millet—that are food staples for

Retaining flood waters until the moment needed for human use remains an essential element of water resource management in all areas— especially South Asia

---

Box 3.2 Tissue culture and marker-aided selection techniques

Most new varieties are the result of tissue culture and marker-aided selection techniques. A rice variety from tissue culture—called La Fen Rockefeller by the Chinese breeder who developed it—is increasing yields by 15–25% for farmers in the Shanghai region. Scientists at the West Africa Rice Development Association have used another culture to cross high-yielding Asian rice with traditional African rice. The result: a new plant type that looks like African rice in its early stages of growth (it grows in dry conditions and can shade out weeds) but becomes more like Asian rice as it reaches maturity, resulting in higher yields with few inputs.

In another breakthrough, scientists announced recently that they have increased the amount of vitamin A in a new variety referred to as "golden rice"—important for reducing vitamin A deficiency, which is a major cause of blindness.

Marker-aided selection is being used in rice to pyramid two or more genes for resistance to the same pathogen, increasing the durability of resistance, and to accumulate several genes, contributing to drought tolerance. For some time to come, this is likely to be the most productive use of biotechnology for cereals.

Source: Conway 1999a.

Box 3.3 The developing world cannot afford to forgo agricultural biotechnology

"Too little attention is paid to the effect of new agricultural technologies on the world's poor and hungry", says Per Pinstrup-Andersen, director general of the International Food Policy Research Institute, in an article summarised here. Most of these people live in developing countries, and they stand to benefit more than anyone from biotechnology. While "Frankenfood" and "terminator seeds" are buzzwords in European media and increasingly in the United States, small farmers in Asia, Africa, and Latin America must wonder what the fuss is about. For them, the heated debate over agricultural biotechnology risks closing off a huge opportunity to improve their lives.

Agricultural biotechnology can help farmers in developing countries produce more—say, by developing new crop varieties that are tolerant of drought, resistant to insects and weeds, and able to capture nitrogen from the air. Biotechnology can also make the foods farmers produce more nutritious by increasing the vitamin A, iron, and other nutrients in the edible part of the plant.

A few private corporations that focus on agriculture in industrial countries, where they expect the highest return on their investment, do most of the biotechnology research. Governments must invest in biotechnology research to help poor farmers, and the public and private sectors must work as partners. The potential of new agricultural technology is enormous, particularly for the poor in developing countries. Condemning biotechnology for its potential risks without considering the alternative risks of prolonging the human misery caused by hunger, malnutrition, and child death is as unwise and unethical as blindly pursuing this technology without the necessary biosafeguards.

Source: International Herald Tribune, 28 October 1999.

---

people in drought-prone regions, who need increased yield stability as much as increased yield.

The growth of transgenic crops, likely to be extremely variable in different parts of the world, has different effects on different continents. In North America transgenic crops already dominate among some crops. In Europe a lack of public acceptance may reduce food imports, causing higher food prices and demand for water to produce food domestically, creating trade conflicts between Europe and North America. In developing countries the adoption of transgenic crops is likely to be highly variable, opening conflicts between governments and private companies with patents for numerous new varieties. The developing world needs to have access to these technologies and to make its own choices (box 3.3).

Increasing storage

Increasing water storage, retaining flood waters until the moment needed for human use, remains an essential element of water resource management in all areas—especially South Asia, where a huge percentage of annual flows are contained in a limited number of floods. The optimum strategy appears to be a combination of storage in aquifers, in tanks and other traditional microstructures, and behind small and large dams.

Building dams

Many large dams—defined by the International Commission on Large Dams (ICOLD) as those higher than 15 metres—are not particularly controversial. The International Hydropower Association estimates that about 300 large dams are currently built every year, not much more than what is required to replace the world's capital stock of 39,000 large reservoirs, and down considerably from the number built in 1960–80.

New dams have become a lot less popular in OECD countries over the past 10–20 years. But about 70% of the hydropower potential in these countries has already been developed, and there is little incentive to increase agricultural areas, other then to increase food exports. Thus the need for more dams is limited. The future of dams in OECD countries is probably as much about decommissioning dams as about building them—about using dams and reservoirs for recreational and environmental purposes as well as for economic development.

- **Recharging groundwater**
- **Harvesting rainwater**
- **Pricing water services**
- **Making managers responsive to users**

New large dams have also become controversial in developing countries, as with the well-known Narmada project in India and the Three Gorges project in China, because of the impacts on the environment and the displacement of people. It is possible to mitigate such impacts, and the dam-building community has done extensive work on possible measures. But the experience with implementing these measures has not persuaded the opponents of dams. Later this year, the World Commission on Dams will produce guidelines on the conditions under which the overall impacts of dams may or may not be beneficial.

Only a small part of the economically feasible hydropower in Africa (6% of 1,000 terawatt-hours a year), Asia (20% of 3,600), and Latin America (35% of 1,600) has been developed (IHA 1999). Countries in these regions may decide that they do not want to develop their hydro potential to the same level as OECD countries (70%). But it is likely that they will decide that the social optimum for hydropower is higher than their current levels of development.

Recharging groundwater

Storing water in aquifers is a compelling solution given the overdrawing of groundwater in China, India, North Africa, the United States, and elsewhere. The threat that overdrawing poses for those who depend on water for their livelihood—and those who depend on the food produced (box 3.4)—is ominous. New techniques and institutional mechanisms are urgently needed to recharge groundwater aquifers. Such mechanisms will include limiting access and providing incentives to users to limit or stop overpumping. The two routes open are to issue permits and control use or to recognise use rights and provide rights holders with incentives to conserve the resource. The second approach is generally more effective.

To make groundwater visible, groundwater protection zones could be created, with special measures for recharge and for reductions on abstraction. All groups affected by the "groundwater rush"—and the ensuing water scarcity, land degradation, water quality loss, and poor public health—need to be enlisted in initiatives to tackle the challenges. They include water user groups, local political leaders and civil society, and politicians and diplomats negotiating with riparian neighbours to reduce abstractions from common groundwater. The media and general public, unaware that this invisible "water savings account" is seriously depleted and under threat, must also be closely involved.

Box 3.4 Groundwater for agriculture

One of the greatest technical revolutions in irrigation has been the development of the small pump. Tens of millions of small pumps are drawing water out of aquifers to irrigate crops. Because pump irrigation provides water on demand, yields from pump irrigation can be two to three times those from canal irrigation. More than half the irrigated area in India is now supplied by groundwater. And since irrigation supplies about half the food produced in India, a third or more of that production depends on these humble devices and the aquifers that feed them.

Much the same is true in other arid countries. Yet almost everywhere in the world, groundwater tables are falling at alarming rates in areas that depend on irrigation from groundwater. In many of the most pump-intensive areas of India and Pakistan, water tables are falling by 2–3 metres a year. This is not surprising: the evaporation losses of a typical crop are around 0.5 metre of water table depth, and the yield of water in an aquifer is about 0.1 metre per metre of depth. Without recharge, groundwater tables would fall by about 5 metres a crop. Most of these areas receive enough rainfall to recharge the aquifers, but most of the rainfall goes to runoff—not to recharge. We desperately need to change that relationship.

It is no exaggeration to say that the food security of China, India, Pakistan, and many other countries in 2025 will largely depend on how they manage groundwater. Reducing pump irrigation is no answer, for that simply reduces the most productive agriculture. The answer has to be in groundwater recharge, not an easy solution. Indeed, no one has devised a cost-effective way to do it on the scale required. About the only plausible idea is to encourage, through subsidies if necessary, flooded paddy (rice) cultivation in lands above the most threatened aquifers in the wet season. Paddy irrigation, with high percolation losses, is inefficient from a traditional point of view. But from the point of view of groundwater recharge, it makes sense. As it turns out, India has been doing precisely this on 180,000 hectares for the past 10 years.

Source: IWMI 2000.

Harvesting rainwater

Rainwater harvesting, generally a socially attractive alternative to large construction, provides opportunities for decentralised, community-based management of water resources. But rainwater harvested upstream reduces the runoff otherwise available to others, or the environment, downstream (unless it would have run to a sink). Nor is harvesting rainwater any more free of environmental costs than taking water from streams for irrigation (box 3.5).

New reservoirs may produce cheap water, but they are expensive in environmental terms. Groundwater provides excellent on-demand storage, but if left unregulated it can easily be overconsumed, affecting other users. Thus, for every alternative, a complete balance of benefits and disadvantages needs to be drawn up. In most cases the best solution will be a combination of surface and groundwater use, with a range of storage options.

Rainwater harvesting provides opportunities for decentralised, community-based management of water resources

Rainwater harvesting has considerable potential for meeting drinking water and irrigation needs in the poor regions of the developing world and for recharging depleted groundwater aquifers. The total rainfall endowment of an area of one hectare in an arid environment with just 100 millimetres annual rainfall is as much as 1 million litres per year.

People on the Indian subcontinent have an ancient tradition of rainwater harvesting. They depend on the monsoon, which brings large quantities of rain in highly concentrated events. Over the years, with community participation in water management taking a backseat, this tradition went into decline. But it is showing signs of revival in areas suffering from acute deforestation and poor land management. These environmental changes have upset the hydrological cycle so much that these areas have become intensely drought-prone.

- In the 1970s two highly ecologically degraded and economically destitute villages—Ralegan Siddhi in Maharashtra (where annual rainfall ranges from 450 to 650 millimetres) and Sukhomajri in Haryana (with annual rainfall around 1,100 millimetres)—took to rainwater harvesting, the first for groundwater recharge, the second for surface storage. With more water available, these villages slowly improved and stabilised their agricultural and animal husbandry outputs and are today food exporters rather than food importers.

- In the mid-1980s Tarun Bharat Sangh, a nongovernmental organisation working in the Alwar district of Rajasthan, encouraged the drought-prone village of Gopalpura to revive its water harvesting tradition of capturing surface runoff. By 1998 the success of Gopalpura had encouraged 650 other villages in the drought-prone district to undertake similar efforts, leading to higher groundwater levels, increased and more stable agricultural incomes, and reduced distress migration.

- With 70 villages building 238 water harvesting structures in one watershed, the 45-kilometre Arvari River—which previously flowed for just a few months during the monsoon season—now flows year round. And the increased groundwater recharge is making life easier for innumerable women living along the river. Village communities along the Arvari River have even formed a River Parliament to regulate use of the river and the groundwater resources of the watershed.

- Impressed by the outstanding achievement of Ralegan Siddhi, Digvijay Singh, chief minister of the state of Madhya Pradesh, replicated the effort in 7,827 villages. Between 1995 and 1998 the project covered nearly 3.4 million hectares of land through a highly participatory watershed development and rainwater harvesting programme. Village watershed committees were created to undertake the programme and turn water management into a people's movement.

- Rainwater harvesting is not just for poor villages. It is being promoted in the Sumida ward of Tokyo to reduce urban floods and in the Indian city of Chennai (formerly Madras) to recharge groundwater aquifers that became saline because of overextraction and seawater. And the latest terminal of Frankfurt Airport—built in 1993—captures 16,000 cubic metres of rainfall from its vast roof for such low-grade water needs as cleaning, gardening, and flushing toilets.

Source: Agarwal 1999.

Reforming water resource management institutions

The biggest challenge in water resource management remains institutional. Political will must change decisionmaking to include all stakeholders, especially women, so that stakeholders have the power to manage their own resources. Public and private management of water can only be improved through greater accountability, transparency, and rule of law.

Pricing water services

As described elsewhere in this report, making water available at low cost, or for free, does not provide the right incentive to users. Water services need to be priced at full cost for all users, which means all costs related to operation and maintenance and investment costs for at least domestic and industrial users. The basic water requirement needs to be affordable to all, but this can be done more effectively than by making all water available to all users at way below cost. Pricing water will provide an incentive for the private sector, large and small, domestic and international, to get involved. It has the potential to provide the dynamics—the funds for research and development, for instance—that the sector lacks.

Making managers responsive to users

Service-oriented management focuses on making managers responsive to user needs. This requires the development of a mutual dependency—such as service for payment—that can take various forms, including service agreements. These provide a detailed description of services to be provided, payments in return for services, verification of service provision, consequences of failing to comply with agreements for both parties, and rules for arbitration of conflict.

The service needs and expectations of users will be influenced by the price they have to pay for those services, especially if they have to pay the full cost. Recognising that services can be provided in different ways using different levels of technology at different levels of cost, service-oriented management thus requires a mechanism to ensure that the services needed by users are provided at the lowest possible cost. Consultation processes, clear service relationships, transparent administration, and accountability mechanisms are among other conditions that have to be put in place for effective service-oriented management.

- **Empowering communities**

- **Restructuring irrigation system management**

- **Valuing ecosystem functions**

- **Increasing cooperation in international basins**

Empowering communities, women, and men

The essence of Vision 21—the sector Vision on water for people—is to put people's initiative and capacity for self-reliance at the centre of planning and action. Water and sanitation are basic human needs—and hygiene is a prerequisite. Recognising these points can lead to systems that encourage genuine participation by empowered men and women, improving living conditions for all, particularly women and children.

Vision 21, in its approach to people-centred development, takes the household as the prime catalyst for change, the first level in planning and management of environmental services. Change in the household or neighbourhood leads to ripples of cooperation and action involving communities and local authorities—and then to actions by district, state, national, and global authorities.

A new alliance of local people, nongovernmental organisations (NGOs), and water agencies can contribute much to achieving the World Water Vision. Community-level action programs could include:

- Watershed action programs in which local people work with NGOs and research organisations to promote conservation and local empowerment.

- Local councils that tackle local problems in water rehabilitation and pollution.

- Basin-level organisations for integrated water management.

- Construction of groundwater recharge wells to improve village water supplies and aquifer management.

- Disaster preparedness linked with community action.

- Drought relief efforts that mobilise work and food supplies.

- Community action in controlling waterborne disease.

- Local action for monitoring water quality, crop selection, and quality control of produce irrigated with effluent water.

Restructuring irrigation system management

Restructuring irrigation systems to provide more benefits to the poor involves a mix of technical and institutional reforms.

Bringing the poor into the dialogue on system priorities can yield new ideas that benefit all stakeholders. New approaches that show potential include:

- *Improving design and operations.* Participatory consultations can reveal inequities in water distribution and possible steps to improve performance. Such consultations can be especially useful during water-scarce periods, when poor and female irrigators may have a particularly hard time obtaining water. For example, flexible cultivation rights can reallocate irrigated land during seasonal water scarcity.

- *Extending new water availability to the poor.* When rehabilitation improves the water supply, new water rights can be given to the poor or those without irrigation. Nepal and Peru offer examples.

- *Linking irrigation management transfer to service improvements.* Irrigation management transfer programmes offer new opportunities for representation for small farmers and women. This participation can result in new water rotations that increase equity between the head and tail ends of an irrigation system and that recognise domestic water needs as a legitimate objective of an irrigation system.

- *Reforming land and water rights.* Some countries have undertaken large-scale redistribution of land and water rights, breaking up large holdings for small farmers and labourers. But the economic and political rationales for such reform are a thing of the past. What is needed is a policy that helps the poor, particularly indigenous groups and ethnic minorities, defend their rights in the context of the water rights consolidation and sectoral transfers emerging from today's economic policies. Where water rights are (re-)distributed, they should be awarded to all users, women and men, landowners and landless farmers.

Valuing ecosystem functions

Water is essential to life, development, and the environment—and the three must be managed together, not sequentially. Because communities rarely understand this interrelationship, awareness raising is the first step. After that, research on the local watershed, public education, and community-led watershed and river basin management can

Many practices adopted to improve the management of water for human needs will also benefit ecosystems

Box 3.6 Estimating the benefits of floodplain use in northern Nigeria

Recent estimates indicate that traditional practices provide greater benefits than irrigation crops on the Hadejia-Jama'are floodplain in northern Nigeria. Firewood, recession agriculture, fishing, and pastoralism generate $32 per thousand cubic metres, compared with $0.15 for irrigation. This evaluation is important because more than half the region's wetlands have already been lost to drought and upstream dams. Thus a proposed increase in water diversion for large-scale irrigated agriculture is inadvisable.

Even without accounting for such services as wildlife habitat, the wetland is more valuable in its current state than after conversion to large-scale irrigated agriculture. The lesson? When cost-benefit analysis includes the value of the goods and services provided by an ecosystem, large-scale development schemes are less profitable than improving the management of the unaltered ecosystem.

Source: Barbier and Thompson 1998.

● Leaving the amount of water in ecosystems required to maintain proper functioning.

● Protecting wetlands and floodplains to enable the benefits from seasonal flooding and provide storage for extreme flood flows.

● Protecting and planting forests in upper catchments, especially in mountainous areas.

● Requiring full effluent treatment by industries and municipalities and applying the "polluter pays" principle.

● Protecting water resources from agricultural runoff.

● Creating groundwater protection zones.

● Rehabilitating degraded areas to recover lost ecosystem functions (through reforestation, wetland restoration, fish population restoration, and so on).

make sustainability possible. As part of the water planning process, each water community should consider how much water to allocate to the natural environment. National legislation should require this, as it does in Australia and South Africa. Decision support models are available, and experience with them should be observed carefully, with a view to applying lessons from elsewhere—taking into account indigenous knowledge and local water management approaches.

Much more research is needed to improve our understanding of ecosystem functioning and to value the services that these systems provide. Recent global assessments of the services provided by freshwater ecosystems (watersheds, aquifers, and wetlands) for flood control, irrigation, industry, recreation, waterway transportation, and the like come up with estimates amounting to several trillion dollars annually (Costanza 1997; Postel and Carpenter 1997). Such knowledge will allow careful assessments of the impacts of water resource use and development on ecosystems, particularly tropical ecosystems (box 3.6). Integration needs to emphasize the river basin as the appropriate scale of management, from the forests in the upper watersheds to the coastal zones affected by the inflows of rivers into wetlands, lagoons, and mangrove ecosystems. The interactions between water resources and coastal zone management are many, but are often ignored or misunderstood (Rijsberman and Westmacott 1997). In the meantime, actions for better-integrated management include:

Many practices adopted to manage water for human needs—rules on extracting and sharing water, changes in cultivation and irrigation to save water for other purposes, returns to ancient and community-based water harvesting and storage—will also benefit ecosystems. Other measures include reducing nutrients through farm-based manure storage, controlling silt by reducing erosion upstream, planning for joint hydropower generation and dry season irrigation, and reducing pollutants from agriculture and industry. Above all, ecosystems will be protected by integrated land and water resource management basin by basin—along with full cost pricing for water services and management reforms for water delivery and wastewater disposal.

Increasing cooperation in international basins

Close to half the world is situated in close to 300 international river basins—rivers that cross national boundaries and whose resources are therefore shared. There are countless examples in history of peoples and countries that have made agreements on how to share such international water resources. There are also ample cases, particularly in times of droughts or rising scarcity, of conflicts over water. In fact, people have been forecasting an increase in wars over water as the ultimate result of such conflicts.

Experience shows, however, that shared water resources *can* be made into a source of cooperation rather than conflict.

- **Stages of successful cooperation**

- **Supporting innovation**

Certainly for a World Water Vision to be realised, the need for cooperation in international basins is paramount. This is not easy, as shown by the 30 years of negotiation needed to reach agreement on the United Nations Convention on the Law of the Non-navigational Uses of International Watercourses. Sadly enough, even after all that time it now seems unlikely that this convention will be ratified by enough countries to enter into force.

It appears that the best we can do is to emphasise how countries get to a better understanding and eventually to deeper cooperation over international waters. There is a series of stages through which most successful cooperation appears to evolve:

● *Confidence building.* Countries that share international rivers usually start with low-level technical cooperation that focuses on exchange of data, or jointly gathered data. International river commissions, with regular meetings of national representatives and a small technical secretariat, often serve this purpose.

● *Cooperation.* As mutual trust and confidence increase, and as issues appear that concern all parties and can be more effectively addressed through collective action, the level of cooperation gradually grows to a point where countries are willing to undertake joint action or allocate more significant resources.

● *International agreements.* After years of successful cooperation, lengthy negotiations are usually required to reach bilateral or regional agreements. Such agreements seldom address the (theoretically desired) comprehensive integrated management of water resources, but focus on specific issues of hydropower, navigation, or environment. Where the interests of upstream and downstream countries diverge sharply over specific issues, it is not unusual that agreement is reached in a wider framework involving cross-border trade or involving other issues that allow agreements in every party's interest.

● *International law and alternative dispute resolution.* Once international agreements have been established, conflicts can be addressed through formal (judiciary, international law) or alternative dispute resolution mechanisms (mediation, arbitration).

Supporting innovation

Because we have a finite amount of water resources and a growing number of people and growing demand, the sustainable use of water ultimately depends on our ability to increase its productivity at least as fast as demand grows. Increasing productivity will depend largely on innovation throughout the sector, through both fundamental research and the widespread dissemination and adoption of its results.

A key part of the necessary innovation will be increased awareness of water issues throughout the population and education and training of people capable of bringing about the necessary changes—that is, capacity building in the water sector. A crucial factor to mobilise resources for capacity building and research will be to give water its proper value. This requires pricing it. Once water is appropriately valued, users and producers will have incentives to conserve it and to invest in innovation. While pricing water is expected to be the primary motivation to bring in the private sector, a host of public goods aspects of water resources will continue to require public funding. These range from researching staple food crops in developing countries to finding cures for tropical diseases—important to populations that do not make up sufficient markets for privately funded research to be attractive.

Notes

1. The background for the work outlined here, the scenarios and modeling done in support of the World Water Vision exercise, is published in a companion volume, *World Water Scenarios: Analysis* (Rijsberman 2000).

2. For fuller treatment of these issues, see the scenarios and models referred to in note 1 and the three main sector Visions, on which much of the following discussion is based: "A Vision of Water for Food and Rural Development" (Hofwegen and Svendsen 1999), "Vision 21: A Shared Vision for Water Supply, Sanitation and Hygiene and a Framework for Future Action" (WSCC 1999), and *Vision for Water and Nature: Freshwater and Related Ecosystems—The Source of Life and the Responsibility of All* (IUCN 1999).

3. Productivity is a better indicator than efficiency. Increasing efficiency at the field or farm level may not have any benefits. And efficiency at the basin level should not necessarily be maximised, because it reduces the amount left over for down-

Increasing productivity will depend largely on innovation through both fundamental research and the widespread dissemination and adoption of its results

stream uses and the environment. Water productivity can be increased by obtaining more production with the same amount of water or by reallocating water from lower- to higher-value crops or from one use to another where the marginal value of water is higher. Indeed, the greatest increases in water productivity in irrigation have not been from better irrigation technology or management, but from increased crop yields due to better seeds and fertilisers (IWMI 2000).

4. Three models were used extensively for the Vision simulations: WaterGAP, developed at the University of Kassel, Germany (Alcamo and others 1999); IMPACT, developed by the International Food Policy Research Institute, Washington, D.C. (Rosegrant and Ringler 1999); and PODIUM, developed by the International Water Management Institute, Colombo, Sri Lanka (IWMI 2000). In addition, the Polestar scenario tool of the Stockholm Environment Institute was used to disaggregate global scenario assumptions to 18 regions.

5. Data for 1995 renewable water resources and use at the country level are from Shiklomanov (1999).

6. The United Nations Medium Scenario, 1998 Revision, is the base for the business as usual scenario (UN 1999). In 2025 more than 80% of the world population—6.6 billion people—will live in developing countries. In addition, the world population will be older and more urban. About 84% of the people in developed countries and 56% in developing countries will live in urban areas, many in megacities (defined as cities with more than 10 million people). The technology, economics, and private sector scenario uses the United Nations Medium Scenario minus 2%. The values and lifestyles scenario uses the United Nations Low scenario.

7. Feedback irrigation systems provide more or less water to fields in response to signals received from farmers concerning their demands, while standard irrigation systems are scheduled to provide water to fields at predetermined times and amounts.

8. Production Scarcity: The country is not physically water scarce, but encounters severe foodgrain deficits because of lack of irrigated area expansion.

Annex

Driver	Business as usual	Technology, economics, and private sector (relative to business as usual)	Values and lifestyles (relative to business as usual)
Demographic			
Population	7.8 billion (6.6 billion in developing countries)	About the same	7.3 billion (6.2 billion in developing countries)
Population growth	1.2% (1.4% in developing countries)	Same or slightly lower (because of higher mortality)	1.05% (1.1% in developing countries)
Urbanisation	61% urbanised (56% in developing countries)	About the same	About the same
Pressures for migration from developing to developed countries	High	Higher (and stronger barriers)	Low
Technological			
Information technology	Widely available and used to increase water management efficiency	Same	Widely available and used to increase water management efficiency and effectiveness
Biotechnology	Widely available and used for new crop varieties	Widely available and used for new crop varieties with high water use efficiency	Widely available and used for new sustainable crop systems and water purification
Water use efficiency	Higher, particularly in arid areas	Dramatically higher	Higher than in business as usual but lower than in technology economics, and private sector
Water pollution	Lower pollution per unit	Lower, mostly in developed and emerging economies	Lower still
New drought-, pest-, and salt-resistant crops	Moderate and controversial	Massive development and dissemination of new varieties, largely solving the agricultural water problem	Same, but combined with ecotechnology and integrated in new agricultural systems
Sanitation	Investment in developing countries grows slower than population	Same	Investment in developing countries grows faster than overall economy; ecotechnology used
Desalinisation	Widely available	Even cheaper	Same
Economic			
Volume of production	$80 trillion ($40 trillion in developing countries)	30% higher, but mostly in developed and emerging economies	$90 trillion ($60 trillion in developing countries)
Structure of production	Gradual dematerialisation; agriculture grows in absolute terms	Little dematerialisation in developing countries; agriculture grows in absolute and relative terms in developing countries	Rapid increase of the nonmaterial economy
Water infrastructure (availability and condition)	Growing at same rate as the economy	Privatised and growing faster than the economy	Growing faster than the economy
Trade	Universal	Some countries or regions excluded from global markets	Universal and strategically regulated
Social			
Lifestyles and cultural preferences	Converge to today's levels in developed countries	Same preferences, but real lifestyles diverge in developed and developing countries	Convergence in developing and developed countries to less material-intensive lifestyles than in today's developed countries
Poverty	Absolute poverty remains constant; relative poverty decreases	Absolute poverty decreases, inequality increases	Absolute poverty eradicated
Economic inequality	High and increasing	Very high and increasing	Gradually reduced
Environmental			
Committed future climate change	Increased variability, agroecologic shifting	Slightly less	Less because of strong emission controls
Water-related disease	Gradually increasing	Gradually decreasing	Only in small pockets
Salinisation	Gradually increasing	Dramatically decreasing	Stopped
Exhaustion and pollution of surface and groundwater	Gradually increasing	Stopped; water withdrawals reduced to sustainable levels	Stopped; water withdrawals reduced to sustainable levels
Integrity and health of aquatic ecosystems	Gradually decreasing	Recovering somewhat	Recovering rapidly
Governance			
Institutions	Insufficient to resolve conflict; severely stressed	Lack of global leadership	Strong and adequate institutions created; shared goals; wide participation
Market dominance	Universal	Same	Universal but regulated
Power structure (international, national)	Asymmetrical but slowly becoming more pluralistic	Increasingly asymmetrical	Much more pluralistic
Conflicts	Ubiquitous and increasing	Same	Practically absent
Globalisation	Accelerating	Accelerating but unequal	Same

Source: Rijsberman 2000.

3

Annex table 3.2 Assumptions for the three World Water Vision scenarios

Variable	Country group/region	Business as usual	Technology, economics, and private sector	Values and lifestyles
Population, 2025	OECD	UN Medium Scenario	UN Medium Scenario	UN Low Scenario
	Medium income	UN Medium Scenario	UN Medium Scenario less 2%	UN Low Scenario
	Least developed	UN Medium Scenario	UN Medium Scenario less 2%	UN Low Scenario
Consumptive water use factor, 2025[a]	All	Can be above 70%	Less than 70%	Less than 70%
Degree of water resource development, 2025[b]	All	Not limited	Not limited	Less than 60%
		Annual total	*Annual total*	*Annual total*
GDP growth, 1995–2000	Western Europe	2.10%	3.32%	1.53%
	Eastern Europe	1.89%	1.42%	4.37%
	CIS	2.15%	2.13%	5.13%
	Aral Sea	2.17%	2.34%	4.50%
	North America	2.10%	3.32%	0.98%
	Central America	1.77%	1.12%	5.18%
	South America	1.95%	1.80%	4.07%
	North Africa	2.06%	4.07%	6.73%
	Southern Africa	1.69%	3.54%	5.20%
	East Africa	1.83%	3.77%	5.92%
	West Africa	1.96%	3.92%	6.11%
	Central Africa	1.92%	3.74%	5.18%
	Middle East	1.40%	1.31%	3.89%
	China	4.20%	4.02%	7.69%
	South Asia	3.49%	3.81%	6.65%
	Southeast Asia	2.98%	3.35%	6.01%
	Japan	0.96%	2.17%	0.12%
	Australia	2.05%	3.27%	1.21%
Growth in irrigated area, 1995–2025	Global	1.5% (0.22% in Brazil, India, and Turkey)	25% IWMI base adjusted	5% IWMI base adjusted
Growth in cereal area, 1995–2025	Global	0.36%	0.31%	0.16%
Growth in irrigated grain yield, 1995–2025	OECD	0.88%	1.50%	1.50%
	Medium income	1.00%	1.80%	2.30%
	Least developed	0.79%	1.00%	2.30%
Growth in rainfed grain yield, 1995–2025	OECD	0.30%	0.60%	0.40%
	Medium income	0.30%	0.45%	0.80%
	Least developed	0.30%	0.30%	1.00%
Growth in irrigation efficiency	OECD	10%	20%	30%
	Medium income	10%	20%	30%
	Least developed	10%	10%	30%

a. Ratio of evaporated water to primary water supply.
b. Ratio of primary water supply to usable water resources.
Source: Rijsberman 2000.

4.

Our Vision of
Water and
Life in 2025

How did the world make so much progress in 25 years?
Five adjustments were crucial. The water crisis became widely recognised.
Land and water resource management became integrated—
with full stakeholder representation. Water services became subject
to full-cost pricing. Innovation and public funding for research increased.
And cooperation in international basins grew.

The year is 2025. Looking around, we see that our efforts begun at the turn of the century are starting to bear fruit. The loss of ecosystem functions and biodiversity has been reversed, and water resources are being rehabilitated. The integrated management of human social and economic activities, with care for catchments and groundwater units, forms the backbone of affordable and sustainable water supplies for communities, farms, and industries.

The world population now stands at 7.5 billion,[1] but everyone has access to safe water supplies. Agriculture produces enough food so that no one need go hungry. Reduced global water consumption by industry has accompanied substantially higher economic activity in what were the emerging and developing countries of 2000. Similar concern for freshwater and the environment has reduced the volume of waste from human activity and led to the treatment of most solid and liquid wastes before their controlled release into the environment.

Some countries lag in their development of representative social and political systems. As a result large parts of the world need further efforts to raise living standards and improve the quality of life for humans and all living things.

People come first...

In 2025 almost every woman and man, girl and boy in the world's cities, towns, and villages knows the importance of hygiene and enjoys safe and adequate water and sanitation. People at the local level work closely with governments and nongovernmental organisations, managing water and sanitation systems that meet everybody's basic needs without degrading the environment. People contribute to these services according to the level of service they want and are willing to pay for. With people everywhere living in clean and healthy environments, communities and governments benefit from stronger economic development and better health.

- **Less disease**

- **Better nutrition**

- **Wiser management**

- **More powerful communities**

- **Higher farm yields**

Many of the water-related diseases rampant at the end of the 20th century have been conquered. Revitalised international efforts to meet people's basic water and sanitation requirements have been combined with effective promotion of hygiene practices. Better primary health care and pollution control have greatly reduced the prevalence and severity of many diseases. Scientists around the world continue to identify links between cancers and chemical contamination of water, along with new methods for preventing and removing the contamination.

Water services are planned for sustainability, and good management, transparency, and accountability are now the standard. Inexpensive water-efficient equipment is widely available. Rainwater harvesting is broadly applied. Municipal water supplies are supplemented by extensive use of reclaimed urban wastewater for nonpotable uses (and even for potable uses in seriously water-short urban areas). On small islands and in some dry coastal areas, desalination augments the water supply. Many cities and towns use low- or no-water sanitation systems, for which communities and local authorities manage the collection and composting services.

Twenty-five years into the new century, all people—both cultivators and those who purchase their food—have access to adequate nutrition, with a minimum national average of 2,750 calories per person a day. Vibrant rural communities feel secure, with education opportunities, social services, and employment opportunities in and out of agriculture. They have reliable access to good transport and communication links with market and administrative centres and with regional and global economies. As a result farmers and other rural residents participate in the global rise in living standards. Agriculture in rainfed, drained, and irrigated areas operates sustainably in an equitable price environment, using water efficiently (box 4.1).

Secure and equitable access to and control of resources—and fair distribution of the costs and associated benefits and opportunities derived from conservation and development— are the foundation of food and water security. Efforts to overcome sector-oriented approaches and develop and implement integrated catchment management strategies continue to be supported by wider social and institutional changes. Many government institutions recognised at the turn of the century the groundwork of grassroots community-based initiatives—and built on this extensively. All new central government policies and legislation are subject to prior

Box 4.1 **A Sahelian future**
Early on an April morning in 2025, on one of the vast floodplains of the Sahel, Ibrahim Diaw leads his herd of long-horned cattle to their dry-season pastures. The grazing routes for nomadic herders follow the areas under an ecosystem restoration programme initiated at the turn of the century. Using these migration pathways no longer results in violent conflicts with farmers, as it did 40 years before when intensive irrigated rice schemes were constructed throughout the plain.
Now Diaw's herd prospers through access to large expanses of restored perennial grasses, including those of the new Wahta Biosphere Reserve. Throughout the wet and dry seasons, water holes provide drinking water for his animals, and the floodplain "works" for the benefit of Diaw and other local people who can count on stable livelihoods based on recession agriculture, semi-intensive production, and artisanal and small-scale commercial fishing.
Diaw walks in the grass and thinks of the past—desiccated flats, 25 years without a single wedding in the villages, his father who thought that they had been forgotten by God. He thinks that efforts to mitigate the impacts of infrastructure development are about to pay off: the dikes have been put to good use, artificial flooding schemes are effective, and water is not wasted anymore.
Source: IUCN 1999.

assessment of their impacts on different stakeholders and beneficiaries. Private and public institutions are today more accountable and oriented towards the local delivery of services and conservation of ecosystems than they were decades ago. They fully incorporate the value of ecosystems services in their cost-benefit analysis and management.

At local levels the empowerment of women, traditional ethnic groups, and poor and marginalised women and men has started to make local communities and weak nations stronger, more peaceful, and more capable of responding to social and environmental needs. Institutional structures, including river basin commissions and catchment committees, actively support the equitable distribution of goods and services derived from freshwater ecosystems. Both husbands and wives are members with voting rights in water user associations in farming communities. Clear property and access rights and entitlements ensure that individuals, companies, and organisations holding those rights meet their associated responsibilities. Enforcement by government regulatory agencies at the local, regional, and national levels is still important for resolving a number of conflicts, such as those between upstream and downstream users.

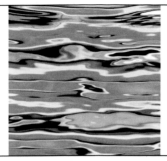

Food and water security requires fair distribution of the costs and associated benefits and opportunities from conservation and development

Extensive field research on water management policies and institutions in developing countries early in the 21st century focused on bringing average yields closer to what was being achieved by the best farmers. Closing the yield gap made the rural livelihoods of poor women and men much more sustainable. Countries that had a basic policy of food self-sufficiency and the capability to implement that policy have increased their yields and production. They did so by increasing the productivity of water through technical and institutional innovation, up to economic and technical limits. China and India are among them.

Because of water shortages, many countries are importing food. The percentage of food traded is about the same as in 2000, with the volume up 30–40%. But there has been a realignment of the countries involved in that trade, with lower-income countries represented to a greater extent. Negotiations on world trade at the beginning of the century paved the way for this. Arid countries, particularly in the Middle East, had a policy of being as self-sufficient as possible, but water limitations kept them from achieving self-sufficiency.

Drawing on technological innovations as well as traditional knowledge, agriculture has made large improvements. Genetically modified crops were initially introduced on a small scale given the lack of public and political support. The biggest advances in food production in the century's first decade were plant improvements through tissue culture and marker-aided selection, crop diversity (especially relying on locally adapted indigenous varieties), appropriate cropping techniques, and soil and water conservation. Now, as the industry has demonstrated its responsibility and gained credibility, use of genetically modified crops is common and has greatly increased the reliability of crops in drought-prone regions.

There has been a 10% increase in water withdrawals and consumption to meet agricultural, industrial, and domestic requirements. Food production has increased 40%. This was possible—in part—because people recognised that water is not only the blue water in rivers and aquifers, but also the green water stored in the soil. Recognition of its crucial role in the water cycle helped make rainfed agriculture more productive while conserving aquatic and terrestrial ecosystems.

Withdrawals for industrial and domestic uses account for half of new withdrawals, due to the high growth in income and consequent demand for water. Only a small percentage of the water delivered to these uses is consumed—most is returned after proper treatment to the ecosystems from which it was drawn. Industrial and domestic water reuse is common, and nonwater-based systems of sewage treatment and other methods of ecosanitation have been applied in many areas to reduce pollution and make full use of human waste as agricultural fertiliser. Seminatural and artificial wetlands are commonly used to improve polluted waters and treat domestic effluents. Countries that faced water scarcities early in the century invested in desalination plants—or reduced the amount of water used in agriculture, transferred it to other sectors, and imported more food.

China, India, Pakistan, and other countries have found it necessary to manage their groundwater better. The answer lay in groundwater recharge. India began doing this in the 1990s through flooded paddy (rice) cultivation in lands above the most threatened aquifers in the wet season. Paddy irrigation has high percolation losses and so is inefficient. But for groundwater recharge, and where water is available at low real cost (excluding subsidies), this apparent inefficiency was just what the doctor ordered. Other countries adopted this approach and others, such as community rainwater harvesting.

Concerns about polluting groundwater through leaching nitrates and other chemicals have also been addressed. Restrictions were placed on fertilisers, pesticides, and other chemicals in groundwater recharge areas after research on maximising the rate of recharge and controlling pollution. Ideally, the recharge areas are not to be used for any other purpose.

At the turn of the century recycling of treated wastewater for agricultural and industrial use was extensively practiced only in Israel, although Tunisia and a few other water-scarce countries were adopting the practice. Today Israel recycles 80% of its wastewater, and it is estimated that nearly half of all municipal wastewater in the world is recycled. This has made a major contribution to meeting the demand for increased consumption.

Rising energy demands in the 21st century have increasingly been met by renewable sources—including large dams in the Zaire basin, where there had been little harnessing of the massive hydropower potential. Many favourable sites are now harnessed, but compensation for environmental, social, and economic impacts has reduced the cost-effectiveness of new projects. In the Mekong River basin, for example, a limited number of dams have been constructed since the 1990s

- **Better management of water resources**
- **Accelerated innovation**
- **More investments in cleaner water and lower use**

because the cost of compensating the millions of fishers in the Tonle Sap wetland and downstream coastal areas made many projects unfeasible. Cheap and effective solar-powered desalination, now widely used in many arid and semiarid countries for domestic water supply, is increasingly affordable.

As forecast in 1999 by the Intergovernmental Panel on Climate Change, the frequency and magnitude of floods and droughts have increased. However, thanks to funding provided early in the century to the international agencies charged with studying the complex processes involved in the water cycle, the causes and patterns are now better understood and measures have been taken to reduce the impact on people and property.

...but we cannot live without the rest of nature

People came to realise that they didn't inherit the earth from their parents—but borrowed it from their children. Water management in 2025 is based on recognising the environmental goods and services that healthy catchments provide. Catchments require constant maintenance, largely provided by local communities, in erosion control, water quality protection, and biodiversity conservation, among other tasks. Strategic or unique natural ecosystems are now highly valued. And conservation programmes, including those for protected areas, usually reflect the needs and involvement of the local communities that depend on them.

Despite concerted efforts and some promising results, contamination of water bodies continues to threaten the environmental security of many societies, in both developed and developing countries. In some areas runoff from agricultural land still affects surface and groundwater resources, though major improvements have come from best management practices and integrated catchment management plans. In other areas contaminants from polluted sediments continue to affect many waterways. Since 2010 investments in the rehabilitation of rivers, lakes, and wetlands have increased, and in many places they now help restore the environmental goods and services these ecosystems provide. Through various means, including artificial wetlands and vegetated buffer strips along riverbanks and lakeshores, domestic effluents and agricultural runoff are controlled and purified.

Empowered communities and individuals, both women and men, regularly participate in all levels of decisionmaking on water resource management (box 4.2). In the United States

> **Box 4.2 For a fair share of clean water**
>
> The community of Asunción Llanque on the Bolivian shores of Lake Titicaca now negotiates every three years with urban and industrial groups and is assured its share of clean water. These groups have established a voluntary code of conduct that has reduced their effluent discharge dramatically since 2015. To ensure a safe water supply to urban areas and factories, the private sector and civil society have invested in conservation and rehabilitation activities in the Lake Titicaca catchment, including soil erosion control, afforestation, and wetland conservation. In many places traditional and innovative mechanisms empower women, men, youth, and the elderly. People from all ethnic groups and social classes now have more equitable access to resources and decisionmaking.
>
> *Source:* IUCN 1999.

in 2000, all states, territories, and tribes had completed unified watershed assessments. Local involvement and coordination with stakeholders was an important element in all assessments. Now more equitable conditions give local communities rights; access to, and control over land, water, and other resources. Laws, markets, and regulations increasingly recognise local people's rights and needs, making possible the sustainable use of natural resources and reconciling livelihood needs with ecosystem functions and requirements.

Innovation in most areas of water resource management—supported by the best of science and traditional knowledge—has accelerated significantly. Innovation also supports development and management for freshwater and related ecosystems. Scientific analysis and modern technologies provide an analytical perspective to problem-solving. Traditional knowledge, the wealth of many generations of water resource management, is also a natural part of decisionmaking and management. The dialogue between scientists and the holders of traditional knowledge formed a cornerstone for many innovative resource management practices.

Investments in cleaner technologies and reduced water and wastewater use continue to help many industries lower their production costs while reducing their effluent taxes. Development investments are based on economic valuations and linked to compliance with the environmental assessment and management standards of the International Standards Organization (ISO) 14000 series. Engineering and construction companies and suppliers adhere to these standards because they provide a clear timeline for infrastructure planning and construction.

4

There is still much to do, but we have made the progress needed to mitigate the water crisis that reigned in 2000 and to advance to sustainable water use and development

Table 4.1 Renewable water use in the World Water Vision

In our Vision the water for irrigated agriculture is drastically limited, with 40% more food produced (partly from rainfed agriculture) consuming only 9% more water for irrigation. Industrial use goes down in developed countries, but the decline is more than offset by increases in the developing world. Municipal use goes up sharply in developing countries, to provide a minimum amount for all, and down in the developed world. Recycling and increased productivity lower the ratio of water withdrawn to water consumed for all uses.

User	Cubic kilometres 1995[a]	Cubic kilometres 2025[b]	Percentage increase 1995–2025	Notes
Agriculture				
Withdrawal	2,500	2,650	6	Food production increases 40%, but much
Consumption	1,750	1,900	9	higher water productivity limits increase in harvested irrigated area to 20% and increase in net irrigated area to 5–10%.
Industry				
Withdrawal	750	800[c]	7	Major increase in developing countries is
Consumption	80	100	25	partly offset by major reduction in developed countries.
Municipalities				
Withdrawal	350	500[d]	43	Major increase and universal access in
Consumption	50	100	100	developing countries; stabilisation and decrease in developed countries.
Reservoirs (evaporation)	200	220	10	
Total				
Withdrawal	3,800	4,200	10	
Consumption	2,100	2,300	10	
Groundwater overconsumption	200[e]	0		Increased recharge of aquifers makes groundwater use sustainable.

Note: Totals are rounded.
a. The 1995 uses are provided for reference. These data are based on Shiklomanov (1999), rounded off.
b. World Water Vision staff estimates.
c. For industry it is recognised that developing countries need a major expansion in industrial water use. For the roughly 2 billion people in cities in developing countries that need livelihoods (both the current poor plus the increase in population) an average of 200 liters a person per day is used. This means a 400 cubic kilometre increase in diversions for industry in developing countries. At the same time, diversions for industry in developed countries can be drastically reduced. Better management and reduced losses lower the ratio of water withdrawn to water consumed.
d. Residential water use of poor people in developing countries needs to be drastically increased. Residential use in developed countries stabilises and is reduced.
e. Postel (1999).
Source: Shiklomanov 1999; World Water Vision staff; Postel 1999.

Governance systems in 2025 facilitate transboundary collaborative agreements that conserve freshwater and related ecosystems and maintain local livelihoods. Management and decisionmaking generally take place at the level where they are most effective and efficient, helping to set up more open dialogue, information exchange, and cooperation. Despite huge efforts, transboundary conflicts are still the most difficult water resource conflicts to resolve in 2025.

There is still much to do, but we have made the progress needed to mitigate the water crisis that reigned in 2000 and to advance to sustainable water use and development (table 4.1).

How we achieved our Vision

How did the world make so much progress in 25 years? Five adjustments were crucial. The water crisis became widely recognised. Land and water resources became systemically managed through an integrated framework. Water services became subject to full-cost pricing. Innovation and public funding for reasearch increased. And cooperation in international basins grew.

Recognition of the crisis and the need for action
In 1987 the Brundtland Commission told the world that our approach to development was unsustainable—but it had lit-

Our Vision of Water and Life in 2025

- **Recognition of the crisis**
- **Stakeholder representation**
- **Full-cost pricing**

tle to say about water. In 1992 the Rio Conference on Environment and Development, in its agenda for the 21st century (Agenda 21), addressed freshwater in chapter 18 of its report. But looking back from 2025, it is clear that the worldwide consultation on water and the environment—the World Water Vision exercise—helped awaken water and environmental professionals and the world public to the crisis in water.

It was known that a few countries were naturally short of water because they were arid. But there had not been a true awakening to the global threat of water stress caused by the rapidly increasing world population and the accompanying rapid increases in water use for social and economic development. Nor had the world truly appreciated the destructive impact that water withdrawals and the discharge of polluted waters were having on freshwater ecosystems.

This changed in 2000. Worldwide consultations shared information and ideas among thousands of water and environmental professionals and civil society representatives. The media of the world seized on the issue as well, raising awareness among decisionmakers and the public. At The Hague in March 2000, under the eyes of the world's media, participants in the Vision exercise and ministers from most countries met to discuss and debate the findings of the consultations and the recommendations of the World Water Commission. The participants launched the movement that made possible the water world that exists in 2025. At the 10th anniversary of the Rio conference, governments, international agencies, the private sector, and nongovernmental organisations announced concrete actions to address a range of water issues.

Stakeholder representation in integrated water resource management

The understanding that all social and economic decisions may have implications for the use of land and water and for the environment had been lost in the society of 2000. Before the industrial revolution, humans lived much closer to nature, understanding that they must live in harmony with it. Some aboriginal peoples retained this understanding in 2000. But the drive to improve economic well-being and security had led to the harnessing of nature for human use, without regard to sustainability.

Urbanisation alienated us even further from nature. Because of the complexities of technology and science, there was specialisation and segmentation of tasks. This created specialised

institutions and cut off communication between specialists about the management of the whole. More important, because the technology of managing water was seen as a task to be left to specialists, ordinary citizens no longer had much of a role in decisionmaking on water management. With the weakness of this approach recognised by many in the 1990s, the World Water Commission underscored the basis for all actions to address the water crisis: integrated management of land and water resources at the basin or catchment level.

Even though the concept of river basin management had been around for decades, there was no ideal model for such an approach in 2000. Basin management was not organised in a way that empowered the residents of the basin with the authority and means to implement their plans. Nor was it always practical or essential to create institutions with administrative boundaries that coincided with watersheds.

Governments approached basin management in different ways. By 2010 most countries had legislation that facilitated community-based activities. Some made it obligatory to develop basin plans for the sustainable use of land and water to be eligible to participate in national economic and social programmes. Because stronger and better public management of land and water was badly needed, some governments reorganised their civil service and streamlined their legislation to reduce the number of agencies with responsibilities in the related sectors and to make them accountable to citizens at the local level. The most effective of these reorganisations started by making redundancy payments to marginal staff.

Most governments adopted legislation that clarified ownership of water or rights to access. In some cases water was declared a public good. Around the world a wide variety of local organisations were developed as appropriate to local circumstances. Among these were some modelled on river basin organisations, others on conservation authorities, and some serving the function of water markets. In 2025 all of them had one thing in common—representative participation by community women and men in decisionmaking. Women professionals trained in the water and environment disciplines in the first decade of the 21st century facilitated women's participation.

Full-cost pricing of water services for all human uses

Full-cost pricing was the most controversial of the World Water Commission's recommendations, for at least three reasons. First, until water began to become scarce in the 1990s,

*Full-cost pricing was the most controversial of
the World Water Commission's recommendations*

it was looked on by many as a free good—a gift from God. Second, governments had long been subsidising the supply of water on the grounds that the poor could not afford it. Third, irrigation water was subsidised to generate employment and keep down the cost of food—again for low-income families, especially in cities.

The reality, of course, is that water is a renewable resource freely available to those on whose land it falls. But in most cases it must be collected, treated, transported, cleaned after use, and returned to watercourses. This requires infrastructure and services that cost something to provide. In addition, when water is scarce, tradeoffs are involved in deciding where it adds the most value, bringing in opportunity costs.

In the world of 2000, with water rapidly becoming more scarce, the Commission agreed with the Dublin principle that to create proper incentives for the management of water, water should be treated as an economic good. But the Commission recognised that full implementation of marginal cost pricing was too big a step to make at that time. Thus it recommended a first step: that the full cost of water services be recovered from users.

This recommendation, including its corollary "the polluter pays", was fairly acceptable to industrial consumers, who could recover the costs as part of the selling price of their products and services. It was also acceptable to communities seeking drinking water services, as they could see that it provided a source of new investments for system extensions to unserved customers. By 2010 public and private utilities were generally applying full cost recovery in these situations. Because some low-income households could not afford water, measures were introduced to subsidise these households so that they could pay for water to meet their basic needs. These households also contributed to the cost of their services in kind through their labour for installation and operation.

It was difficult to sell the concept that customers should pay the full cost of urban sewerage, because it was often perceived that the beneficiaries included others beyond those connected to the system. Sanitation was seen to have some public good characteristics, along with such water-related services as flood management—and both continued to require public financing (box 4.3).

It was much more difficult to sell the concept of paying the full cost of irrigation water. Yet it was critical that this water be

> **Box 4.3 Social Charter for Water**
>
> At the Second World Water Forum in March 2000, the French NGO Académie de l'Eau presented a Social Charter for Water. Based on a series of successful experiences identified by research and over a website over a period of months preceding the forum, the charter proposed a series of measures for community water mangement. When implemented simultaneously, those measures made it possible to organise the beneficiaries of water supplies to inform and sensitise them to issues of water management, educate them on possible solutions, and thus prepare them to work with water professionals to address their needs.
>
> Académie de l'Eau also provided a toolbox of concrete actions and measures. And with its associates it launched a small fund with contributions from water utilities in the developed world to assist communities that wanted to test these approaches, increasing the scope of experiences from which to learn. The approach was first employed in the francophone countries of Africa, but through regional and worldwide networks it contributed much to the community movement throughout the world.
>
> *Source:* World Water Vision staff.

valued, because it represented the bulk of water diverted for human needs. In 2000 suppliers of irrigation water (generally government agencies) were not even recovering most operation and maintenance costs. As a first step governments had begun decentralising responsibility for operation and maintenance to cooperatives or to private owners—a trend accelerated in the first years of the new century. Because farmers depended on the proper functioning of these systems for their livelihoods, they ensured operation and maintenance. Again, many farmers and especially lower-income users contributed their services as in-kind contributions to the cost. Appropriate low-cost technology such as treadle pumping of shallow groundwater was widely adopted for holders of small plots. All operation and maintenance subsidies were eliminated.

Indirect subsidies to operating costs, such as energy, were also eliminated. This had a major impact on water management in India, which in 2005–15 discouraged groundwater overpumping by gradually eliminating subsidies for the energy to pump water from wells.

New water storage facilities were built in the first 25 years of the century for irrigated agriculture and industrial water, as well as for recharging groundwater aquifers. Governments awarded more contracts to private operators to build, own, and operate these facilities, with awards going to those requiring the lowest transparent government subsidies.

Our Vision of Water and Life in 2025

- **More public funding for research and innovation**

- **Increased cooperation in international basins**

A new round of negotiations of the World Trade Organization in 2010 agreed to add water subsidies to the list of unacceptable subsidies to inputs for agriculture. As this policy was implemented in the years that followed, food prices from exporting countries rose slightly, improving farm incomes in developing countries. Prices eventually stabilised around their previous level, but low-income urban dwellers felt the pinch of higher food prices while they lasted.

The move to full-cost pricing was coupled with a continuing strong government presence in establishing and managing frameworks of regulatory policies and laws that provided long-term stability. This attracted badly needed infrastructure investments by local and international private businesses. At the same time, investments in public goods and subsidies targeted to low-income water users added to public budget expenditures. Government budgets related to water remained more or less at the levels of 2000 throughout the first quarter of the century. Costs now carried by consumers and the private sector were replaced by investments in public goods, subsidies to low-income women and men, and publicly funded research and development.

More public funding for research and innovation

At the turn of the century there was a dearth of innovative thinking and new technologies for water management, unlike the case for informatics and pharmaceuticals. The Commission realised that the likely cause was that water had not been valued and thus was of little interest to the private sector. Pricing water would eventually spark interest in the sector, but this might take time—and some research areas might never be of interest to the private sector. So the Commission encouraged governments to publicly fund such research, a process that bilateral donors and private foundations helped kickstart in 2000 when they committed to provide funds for water-related research in national laboratories in developing countries, using the model developed by the Consultative Group on International Agricultural Research.

At the turn of the century practitioners knew that urban environmental sanitation needed alternatives to traditional waterborne waste disposal. Pilot projects were implemented in 2000, with a network sponsored by the Global Water Partnership ensuring that experiences were shared. By 2010 communities were applying these lower-cost and more environmentally friendly approaches not only in low-density urban areas and perimeters but also in cities. Also in 2010 hyper-accumulating plants were bred to take toxins out of

soil. Through biotechnology, micro-organisms in the soil were used to remove pollutants from groundwater.

In an unexpected development in 2015, a Canadian research institute developed a strain of grain that had stalks more digestible by animals. The adoption of this strain by such countries as India, then using 500 million tons of cereal residues a year as livestock feed, had a tremendous impact on the feed grain required—and freed up water for other crops for humans. Laboratory work continued on molecular genetics. And there was enough public confidence that field trials had been completed for genetically modified plants combining drought resistance with high yields.

As a result of continuing reductions in the cost of information and communication technology, farmers could manage water and other inputs better—using global positioning systems, satellite connections, and remote-sensing data for precision farming. Using indigenous knowledge, national agricultural institutes were adapting such technologies to the needs of the location and the people in 2015. Qualified local consultants were able to use this information and technology to provide services to farmers at a fraction of what foreign consultants had charged in the previous century. All but subsistence farmers could now afford this technology.

Information technology also offered tremendous opportunities for the way water resource knowledge is distributed and used. By 2010 the large amounts of water-related information on the Internet were managed by networks of experts and resource managers, who categorised it and distributed regular updates on, for example, contacts, projects, laws, methods, tools, and best management practices.

Hydrological data were routinely collected under the guidance of the revitalised United Nations Agency Coordinating Committee's Subcommittee on Water Resources. Initiatives to share the data became widespread, forming the basis for new or updated bilateral and multilateral water-sharing agreements. Environmental data and the underlying understanding of environmental processes were also widely shared, communicated in terms suitable for use in education and public information campaigns and, most important, for river basin management.

In 2000 water resource managers were beginning to understand ecological functions and services. But when they tried to quantify the concepts for use in water resource management

People came to realise that they didn't inherit the earth from their parents— but borrowed it from their children

calculations, they found that very little was known. As a first step, countries recognised that discharge of all pollutants and contaminants to the environment must be minimized. The World Water Forum in The Hague launched research projects to obtain relevant data on the interaction of the water cycle and ecosystems for a variety of geographic and climatic conditions. And the research activities that supported integrated catchment management increased sharply after 2000.

By 2010 scientists from many developing countries had made major innovative contributions to freshwater resource management using funds for local research provided by donors and concepts for innovative water policies and institutions developed by the International Water Management Institute in Sri Lanka. This helped develop local capacity so that by 2015 project implementation depended far less on technical expertise from developed countries. Now in 2025 the minimal water requirements of most flora and fauna in wetlands and rivers are well known and used in planning and managing water resources.

At the turn of the century concern for the environment showed up only in environmental statements, impact assessments, and environmental action plans that were annexes to traditional water resource management plans. In 2000 the United Nations Educational, Scientific, and Cultural Organzation's (UNESCO) International Hydrological Programme began coordinating the teaching of these subjects to change this duality of thinking. It took a generation to train academics, professional teachers, and trainers at the new UNESCO Water Resources Capacity Building Institute in Delft, the Netherlands. But by 2015 environmental awareness was an integral part of engineering and water resource management practices.

As a result of similar training for primary and secondary school teachers, combined with more widespread access to education, children in 2015 were leaving school aware of the interconnectedness of their actions and the environment. Education and awareness programmes—such as *Water, the Source of All Life* and *Our Catchments, Our Wealth*—have sharply increased public understanding of ecosystem goods and services and general recognition of the need for water to maintain them. The greater education and awareness have

become the impetus for broader public involvement. The view is now common that collective decisions should give due consideration not just to the next generation but to many future generations as well. And that view forms the basis for much of the discussion in catchment committees.

Increased cooperation in international water basins

In May 2000 not enough nations had ratified the United Nations Convention on the law of the Non-navigational Uses of International Watercourses to bring it into force, after taking more than 25 years to draft it and after the General Assembly adopted it almost unanimously. Although the principle seemed sensible, almost every national government found it either too strong or too weak—with positions often appearing to depend on whether a nation was upstream (too strong) or downstream (too weak) in international basins.

The Commission recommended that governments voluntarily accept the limitation of their sovereign rights to permit consultations and decisions based on integrated water resource management at the basin level. Some countries objected. Others were already applying the principle, and countries from the Middle East and from the Nile basin made presentations at the Second World Water Forum describing their cooperative efforts.

As more nations and communities applied the principle in their watersheds, it became clear that it was the right approach. It was only a short step to apply the approach to international basins, accepted in almost all international watercourses by 2020, when a new international convention codifying the principles and specifying dispute resolution mechanisms was ratified by countries of the United Nations.

Note

1. In the scenarios explored in chapter 3 world population in 2025 ranges from 7.3 to 7.8 billion. In our Vision we have assumed that increasing prosperity will continue the trend towards lower popuation growth—and used 7.5 billion people for 2025.

5.

Investing for
the Water Future

We are all stakeholders when it comes to water.
If each of us assumes the responsibility to act, we will start a
movement to bring about our Vision

The World Water Vision has three primary objectives: to empower women, men, and communities to decide how we use water, to get more crops and jobs per drop, and to manage use to conserve freshwater and terrestrial ecosystems. It also specifies five actions critical to their achievement: involving all stakeholders in integrated management, moving to full-cost pricing for all water services, increasing public funding for research and innovation, cooperating to manage international basins, and massively increasing investments in water. Responsibility for implementing this Vision belongs to all of us: to governments; to multinational agencies; to women and men in households, communities, nongovernmental organisations (NGOs), academia, and research institutes; and to the private sector. The activities to implement the Vision are grouped here under four headings: policies, institutions, research and development, and investments (see page 62).

As the Vision exercise proceeded, the Global Water Partnership initiated a process to determine concrete actions to implement the Vision strategy. The Framework for Action Unit has been working closely with sectors and regional groups to develop action plans and investment requirements. Before the Second World Water Forum in The Hague in March 2000, the unit will have produced a framework for action that describes the main elements of that plan, available for discussion and debate in the forum, along with the Commission findings and the many Vision documents prepared through the consultations.

Closing the resource gap

Agenda 21, the report of the 1992 Rio Conference on Environment and Development, placed the additional investment cost of achieving global water security at $56 billion a year. The Vision 21 report (WSSCC 1999), based on consultations organised by the Water Supply and Sanitation Collaborative Council, estimated that if more appropriate technologies were used, the costs for water supply and sanitation would be only $225 billion, in addition to the costs borne

- **Water and sanitation's needs**

- **Industry's needs**

- **Environment's needs**

- **Agriculture's needs**

by households and communities. Yet in the European Union alone it is estimated that $150–215 billion is needed to achieve sewerage compliance by 2010. In the United States the American Water Works Association estimates that investments in drinking water infrastructure over the next 20 years will be about $325 billion, with $12 billion to protect sources. The Water Environment Federation estimates that $325 billion will be required over the same period for pollution control, with $200 billion for treating sanitary sewer overflows.

When the needs of the rest of the world are also considered, it is clear that very large investments will be required. The world population is projected to increase by 1.5 billion people by 2025, roughly half of them in cities. Another 0.75 billion people will move to cities. About 2 billion urban dwellers already live without sanitation. At a conservative estimate of $50 a person for urban water supply and sanitation, the cost of supplying 3.5 billion people will be nearly $1.8 trillion.

None of these numbers includes the cost of industrial water supply and treatment. By 2025 annual industrial water withdrawals will have increased by 50 cubic kilometres, equivalent to the average water consumption of 1 billion people. Indeed, the growth in industrial use in developing countries will be twice this amount, partly offset by lower use in developed countries. Industrial waste is often more expensive to treat than sewage. It would seem reasonable to assume that the investment in industrial water supply and wastewater treatment will be equivalent to that for urban water supply and sanitation—that is, a second $1.8 trillion. This assumption is conservative if one considers the needs to treat the industrial wastewater now discharged without treatment (including cooling towers for thermal energy plants) and to clean polluted land and water bodies.

By 2025 annual withdrawals for irrigation, under our Vision, will increase by 150 cubic kilometres. Related works would cost about $225 billion, with $75 billion for storage and the remainder for irrigation infrastructure through to tertiary systems. We have assumed that the remaining increase in food production will come from more productive use of water in existing agriculture (especially research, management, and technologies to increase the productivity of water in both rainfed and irrigated agriculture). Without knowing more precisely what these measures will be, it seems reasonable to

assume that this would cost about the same ($225 billion). Additional storage capacity of 200 cubic kilometres will be needed to replace unsustainable groundwater overconsumption at a rough cost of $100 billion. This would bring the total cost to $550 billion to produce 40% more food (assessed as required to end hunger) and employment in rural areas.

None of these numbers provides for the replacement of existing systems because of age, neglect, or both.

Pending the completion of the cost estimates to be prepared at the regional level to accompany the Framework for Action, total investments are conservatively taken to be $4.5 trillion over 30 years, or $150 billion a year for 1995–2025. Since these added investments were not made in 1995–2000, the estimate for 2000–25 is even higher. Here we have used $180 billion (table 5.1). It must be emphasized that these are estimated investments in new works.

For surface water storage alone, about 1% of the installed capacity of 6,000 cubic kilometres will need to be replaced each year through new construction or dredging, at a rough cost of $30 billion a year. The estimates assume that operation and maintenance costs will be covered by existing revenue structures, even though this is seldom the case for irrigation systems today.

Table 5.1 Annual investment requirements for water resources

Investments have to increase by more than $100 billion a year—with less for agriculture and more for industry and the environment.

Use	Billions of U.S. dollars		Share (%)	
	1995	Vision 2025	1995	Vision 2025
Agriculture	30–35	30	43–50	17
Environment and industry	10–15	75	13–21	41
Water supply and sanitation	30	75	38–43	41
Total	70–80	180	100	100

Source: World Water Vision staff.

There is a role for all investor groups in meeting the financing challenge

Mobilising new financial resources

Total investment in water services today—excluding that directly by industry as part of establishment costs—is estimated at $70–80 billion a year. The largest investor in services is government—the traditional public sector, which contributes about $50 billion a year. The private sector, ranging from small water vendors to private municipal and metropolitan utilities, contributes around $15 billion. International donors contribute a further $9 billion for both water and sanitation services and irrigation and drainage. An investment newcomer—the international private sector—contributes about $4 billion a year.

There is a role for all investor groups in meeting the financing challenge (box 5.1). The domestic private sector, already active and important in many places, offers great additional resource potential. At one end of the scale this includes sanitary wares such as latrines, water carts, and carriers; at the opposite end, major manufacturers and service delivery companies. Local consultants can be as qualified as much more expensive foreign consultants—and have a better understanding of local conditions. At one end of the scale in food production are water storage and harvesting devices and micro-irrigation equipment. At the other end are agroindustrial equipment manufacturers supplying major irrigation schemes. As noted, industry should also finance its own water supply and wastewater treatment facilities—or make capital contributions to installations that meet the needs of municipalities and large industry.

Proven social mobilisation approaches must be used more to engage the resources of those not served by water and sanitation systems. That may require subsidies. But it mainly requires the recognition that traditional central finance has simply not provided water and sanitation to all women and men. The value of the community approach has been demonstrated in the construction of water harvesting schemes in the Alwar District of Rajasthan (box 5.2).

Great hopes have been expressed for major investments by the international private sector: a recent stockbroker report suggested that an increase to $100–165 billion is achievable. If governments accept the World Water Commission's recommendation of full-cost pricing for water services, this will be a great incentive not only for local investors but also for international private investment. Attracting this investment will also require good water governance—strong regulations, sound policies, and up-to-date laws.

Box 5.1 Examples of resource mobilisation actions

- Close the resource gap for provision of water services (treatment, supply, environmental protection) of $100 billion or more a year.

- Mobilise new investment from the international private sector.

- Integrate service development with the local consumer economy to create enterprises and jobs based on water services and wares.

- Develop pricing and charging schemes that ensure the financial sustainability of water investments.

- Gain recognition for water investments among the ethical investment community—*Blue Funds* to complement *Green Funds*.

- Facilitate poor countries' access to water funds and develop microcredit mechanisms—such as the Grameen Bank in Bangladesh—for use at the community level, to support women and disadvantaged groups.

- Encourage local development banks (agricultural and industrial) to lend at concessional rates for water-related programmes.

- Enable developing countries to attract and benefit from private sector funds by having donors focus on institutional strengthening.

- Make concessional multilateral funds available for water supply and sanitation investments only in countries that have adopted the recommended policy and institutional changes.

- Ensure that water services are recognised for their contribution to poverty alleviation—enabling governments to use funds released by debt relief for water services.

Source: Global Water Partnership 2000.

Box 5.2 Water harvesting costs in India

Where Indian communities have taken up water management themselves, they have ensured that the total investment costs were low and contributed substantially to these costs. Tarun Bharat Sangh, an NGO, has been working with more than 500 villages in the Alwar district of Rajasthan, encouraging them to build through their own efforts almost 2,500 water harvesting structures. These villages have contributed as much as 92% to the total cost of these structures—and, with the success of these efforts, the share of village contributions has been increasing.

In 1997–98 the total investment in the water harvesting structures was 150 million rupees, with 110 million from the villagers. The structures built by the village communities are extremely low cost—ranging from 0.2 rupees ($0.0004, or four-tenths of a cent) per cubic metre of storage capacity to 3 rupees ($0.07). No engineering organization, public or private, can match these costs for storage.

Source: Agarwal 1999.

Activities to implement the Vision strategy

Stakeholder	Policies	Institutions
International organisations, including private foundations	Promote social and financial solidarity by sharing information on efforts to reduce the growing gap in access to safe water and environmental services between the rich and poor. Promote transparency, accountability, and participation. Promote precautionary principle in management of water risks.	Promote stable and fair food markets through the World Trade Organization. Reform, strengthen, and provide more resources to the United Nations Agency Coordination Committee, Subcommittee of Water Resources (ACC-SWR). Coordinate reform of water resource education to integrate environmental concerns through the International Hydrological Programme.
Governments, including government agencies and universities	Facilitate mechanisms to allow management of land and water at the basin and catchment levels. Adopt formal policy of full-cost pricing of water services. Empower communities to develop their own water and sanitation systems based on their needs and willingness to pay. Devise incentives (including pricing) to encourage sustainable water use. Develop regulations that encourage the private sector while protecting the interests of society. Accept limited sovereignty over water in international watercourses.	Dispel idea that water management is primarily a government responsibility. Review structure and coordination mechanisms between water agencies to avoid conflicts and inefficiencies. Promote transparency, accountability, and rule of law in all institutions. Assign responsibility and resources for municipal water supply and sanitation to the city or community level. Establish participatory market processes for water allocation.
Private sector, local and international	Be responsible to society as well as to shareholders.	Foster community representation in corporate governance structure. Include an ethics subcommittee.
Nongovernmental organisations and communities	Accept primary responsibility for water; be guardians of water resources; delegate upward only what cannot be managed locally (subsidiarity principle).	Participate in management of water supply and irrigation schemes.

Research and development	Investments	Stakeholder
International water and environmental standards setting and national monitoring, with ACC-SWR in the lead and with biannual reporting through World Water Development Report.	Training and education on integrated water resource management.	International organisations, including private foundations
	International monitoring of water availability, quality, and productivity.	
Innovative research of institutional and technological approaches to better water management.	Provide loans only when sustainable integrated water resource management policies are in place.	
Nationally adapted water research management programmes.	Capacity building, including redundancy payments for marginal staff and appropriate salary structure for public agencies.	Governments, including government agencies and universities
National laboratory testing and certification of safe biotechnology for food production and waste treatment.	Public goods such as flood protection, with the public sharing pollution control costs.	
Systematic data collection and reporting on water resource availability, renewal rates, quality, and uses.	Targeted subsidies to low-income and disadvantaged groups to satisfy basic needs for water, sanitation, and hygiene.	
Extensive training and credit systems for small holder farms.		
Water-saving technologies.	Urban water supply and domestic and industrial wastewater treatment.	Private sector, local and international
Desalination.	Irrigation systems.	
Safe biotechnology for food production and waste treatment.	Water storage.	
Regional and global networking to share community-based solutions.	Rainwater harvesting.	Nongovernmental organisations and communities
	Household-based water supply and sanitation.	
	Community microcredit schemes.	

Investing for the Water Future

- **Sources of water resource investments**

- **Launching a movement**

Table 5.2 Sources of water resource investments

These are investment costs for new infrastructure only. Cash-flow calculations will require adding provisions for replacement costs and operation and maintenance.

Source	Billions of U.S. dollars		Share (%)	
	1995	Vision 2025	1995	Vision 2025
National				
Public sector	45–50	30[a]	58–71	25
Private firms	12–15[b]	90[c]	15–21	45
International				
Private investors	4[b]	48	5–6	24
Donors	9	12	12–13	6
Total	70–80	180	100	100

a. Government will need to maintain their annual budgets at $50 billion to include direct subsidies to the poor who otherwise will not be able to afford the cost of accessing services provided by these investments.

b. Does not include investments by industry.

c. Includes investments by industry, excluding hydropower.

Source: World Water Vision staff.

Using the investment funds effectively and minimising the risks of exploitation by public agencies and local and foreign companies will require openness, transparency, stakeholder involvement, and efficient local management. When this happens, the local private sector will also take a greater interest—and since it will feel more at home with the risks, it will be a greater source of investment than international companies.

Private actors can thus provide the main source of infrastructure investment (table 5.2). Government resources will contribute a smaller share in direct capital investment and maintenance costs for traditional water supply projects. This will free up public and softer loan and grant resources for water-related projects that supply public goods (such as flood management) and for subsidies to low-income and disadvantaged women and men to pay the cost of their minimum water, sanitation, and irrigation needs. This explicit subsidy element accounts for the need for total government cash flows to remain at current levels. The key role of government is to provide a regulatory and policy framework for investments to ensure financial sustainability—investments based on social equity and other guiding principles in the national water policy.

Donors need to provide strategic assistance in developing policies, regulations, institutional capacity, human resources, and the technical and scientific competencies required to manage the resource base and water services in a fully integrated fashion. Donors are also important in helping countries provide for basic needs and environmental protection. The Global Environment Facility, for example, could be expanded to make even more funds available to support environmental research, the conservation of freshwater biodiversity, and the management of international waters and coastal areas. It is recommended that donors continue to support integrated management and social and noncommercial uses of water.

All investors can help meet the goal of doubling investment, with the balance among them to vary by region and by country. So far, most international private flows have gone to Asia and South America. Donors must direct funds to supporting the poorest countries, particularly in Africa and South Asia. The key is to identify each donor's role so that donors can operate in synergy rather than competition to produce the best result.

Launching a movement

In every country and for every activity concerning water and the environment, waste, authoritarian practices, and duplicated or fragmented efforts result in high transaction costs and misallocated resources. International systems are just as inefficient.

What can change this? Both public and private management of water will improve through greater accountability, transparency, and rule of law. Incentives must improve for all stakeholders. More community participation will provide a sense of ownership and empowerment to local stakeholders. The role of education in making this process possible cannot be overestimated. Public access to information will provide an incentive to elected officials and private operators, who will be held responsible for results, including maximising social welfare. It will also reduce opportunities for corruption and for the capture of the system by powerful elite. And it will increase opportunities for civil servants to be better trained, better equipped, and better paid.

At The Hague in March, stakeholders from around the world—politicians, civil servants, water and environmental professionals, NGOs representing communities, youth, women, and special interest groups—came together to

Both public and private management of water will improve through greater accountability to users, transparency, and rule of law. The role of education in making this process possible cannot be overestimated

debate the issues and recommendations in this report. They met in sessions of the Second World Water Forum, a Ministerial Conference, and a World Water Fair. Each of these stakeholders—we are all stakeholders when it comes to water—will be asked to make a commitment to specific actions to start to create the water world we envision for 2025. If each of us assumes the responsibility to act, we will start a movement to bring about our Vision.

Appendix

Terms of reference

Chairman and members

Vision management

Partner organisations

Meetings and consultations

Background documents

terms of ref

Terms of reference for the World Water Commission

The First World Water Forum in Marrakech in March 1997 mandated the World Water Council to develop a *World Water Vision*. The Marrakech declaration identified the process to develop the *Vision* as "building on past international efforts and relying on the collective wisdom and resources of the global community. The process leading to the Vision will include research, consultations, workshops, print and electronic publications, and many other means for absorbing, synthesising, and disseminating knowledge. At the conclusion of this process, fully aware of the pitfalls along the way, the Vision will offer relevant policy and region- and country-specific conclusions and recommendations for action to be taken by the world's leaders to meet the needs of future generations".

Several steps and actions have already been taken to initiate the process and to meet this challenge in cooperation with several organisations worldwide. The International Conference on Water and Sustainable Development held in Paris in March 1998 was one such activity towards developing the *Vision* and fulfilling the mandate given to the World Water Council in Marrakech. At this meeting the Council presented two documents:

● The background document "Water in the 21st Century"

● The "Proposed Framework for the *Long-term Vision for Water, Life and the Environment*".

The Final Declaration of this ministerial conference encouraged the World Water Council to proceed with its work. The current Vision exercise is based on the Framework document.

At a brainstorming meeting held in Washington, D.C., in July 1998, the idea of forming a World Commission on Water for the 21st Century was born, and the Commission was formed under the Chairmanship of Dr. Ismail Serageldin, Chairman of the Global Water Partnership, Governor of the World Water Council, and Vice President of the World Bank. The Commission is being co-sponsored by the World Health Organization, United Nations Educational, Scientific, and Cultural Organization, United Nations Department for Social and Economic Affairs, United Nations Development Programme, Food and Agriculture Organization, United Nations Environment Programme, United Nations University,

World Meteorological Organization, and World Bank. The creation of the Commission was announced in Stockholm on August 11, 1998.

Goals and objectives

The goals of the *Commission* are to make recommendations on how to:

● Ensure food security through aquaculture, and rainfed and irrigated agriculture;

● Provide adequate water supply and sanitation services;

● Develop water resources for economic uses, including industrial water uses, energy production, navigation, and tourism and recreation; and

● Preserve essential environmental functions with increased emphasis on sustaining our ecosystems.

The Commission is to guide and report on the findings of the Vision exercise, whose objectives are to:

● Develop knowledge on what is happening in the world of water regionally and globally, and on trends and developments outside the world of water which may affect future water use;

● Based on this knowledge, produce a consensus on a Vision for the year 2025 that is shared by water sector specialists and decisionmakers in the government, the private sector, and civil society;

● Raise awareness of water issues among the general population and decisionmakers in order to foster the political will and leadership necessary to achieve the Vision; and

● Utilise the knowledge and support generated to influence the investment strategies of countries and funding agencies.

Process

The Vision exercise will be conducted over a period of a year and a half—roughly from September 1998 to March 2000. The Commission will establish Thematic Panels to focus expert attention on trends outside the water sector and a Scenario

Development Panel to assist the consultative process. Day-to-day activities will be managed by a Vision Management Unit operating from UNESCO in Paris and World Water Council offices in Montreal. A *first round of Consultation* will sensitise and draw upon the knowledge of water sector organisations. *Subsector Visions* will be developed through cooperation with established organisations. *Regional Visions* will be developed for areas where water issues are, or are expected to become, particularly pressing. The results of these discussions will be synthesised into a draft Vision. A *second round of Consultation* will then be held, including discussions at the 1999 Stockholm Symposium, before the Vision is finalised and presented at *the Second World Water Forum and Ministerial Conference* scheduled for World Water Day 2000, March 17–22, in The Hague. This event is a unique opportunity to convert public awareness on water into political commitment.

The Commission will carry out its work with total independence, guided by these Terms of Reference. It will be supported by the Vision Unit, who will coordinate the exercise on a day-to-day basis under the guidance of the Chairman of the Commission, who will have the close collaboration and support of the Vision Management Committee established by the World Water Council.

Meetings

The Commission will conduct most of its work by correspondence and through the participation of individual members in *Vision* activities. For example, they will receive for comment various draft documents, including the work plan of the exercise and draft terms of reference for key elements thereof. The full Commission will meet on two occasions prior to issuing its report. The first meeting will be in Cairo on March 23,

1999. The second will be in Stockholm on August 9–10, 1999. The third meeting will be when the Report is released to the world at the Second World Water Forum in The Hague, March 22, 2000.

At the first full meeting (in Cairo) the Commission will review progress made by the Vision exercise up to then, and plans for its continuation. Commission members will provide their advice on the work plan. They will also comment on the outline of the subject areas to be covered by the report of the Commission. At the meeting in Stockholm the Commission will discuss a report on the findings of the first round of sector and regional consultations as summarised and integrated by the Vision Unit. Members will also discuss and give direction on the content of the Commission's report. The Commission will finalise its report mainly through correspondence.

Leading an international reflection

The process to be followed by the Vision exercise is one that will bring together networks of existing institutions. To the extent possible it will begin a participatory process open to all professionals and all water users, in particular women, people living in poverty, and disadvantaged groups. Special efforts will be made to reach out to women and youth. The whole Vision exercise will be a start of a process in which people talk to each other who have not always done so in the past. It will encourage water professionals and others to think about possibilities they have not always considered in the past. It will lead to scenarios and a Vision of the future for the management of water that will lead to policies and investments that avoid pitfalls and take advantage of opportunities. Members of the Commission will play key roles as visionaries and spokespersons throughout this international consultation.

Appendix

Chairman of the World Water Commission

Ismail Serageldin, Vice President, World Bank, and Chairman, Consultative Group for International Agricultural Research and Global Water Partnership

Honorary members

HRH The Prince of the Netherlands
Norman Borlaug, Nobel Laureate, United States
Hon. Ingvar Carlsson, Former Prime Minister of Sweden
Jean Dausset, Nobel Laureate, France
Hon. Mikhail Gorbachev, Former President of the Former USSR
Henry Kendall, Nobel Laureate, United States [deceased]
Hon. Sir Ketumile Masire, Former President of Botswana
Hon. Fidel Ramos, Former President of the Philippines

Members

The countries listed reflect the nationality of the commissioners, not the location of their organisation.

Shahrizaila bin Abdullah, Malaysia (Hon. President, International Commission on Irrigation and Drainage)
Anil Agarwal, India (Director, Centre for Science and the Environment)
Abdel Latif Al-Hamad, Kuwait (Chairman of the Board, Arab Fund for Economic and Social Development)
Kader Asmal, South Africa (Professor and Chairman of the World Commission on Dams; Minister of Education of South Africa)
Asit Biswas, India (President, Third World Center for Water Management)
Margaret Catley-Carlson, Canada (International Consultant; Former President, Canadian International Development Agency and Population Council)
Gordon Conway, United Kingdom (President, Rockefeller Foundation)
Mohamed T. El-Ashry, Egypt (Chairman and Chief Executive Officer, Global Environment Facility)
Howard Hjort, United States (Former Deputy Director-General, Food and Agriculture Organization)
Enriqué Iglesias, United States (President, Inter-American Development Bank)

Yolanda Kakabadse, Ecuador (President, World Conservation Union)
Speciosa Wandira Kazibwe, Uganda (Vice President, Uganda)
Jessica Mathews, United States (President, Carnegie Endowment for International Peace)
Robert S. McNamara, United States (Co-Chair, Global Coalition for Africa)
Jérome Monod, France (Chairman of the Supervisory Board, Suez Lyonnaise des Eaux)
Peter Rogers, United Kingdom (Division of Engineering and Applied Sciences, Harvard University)
Maurice Strong, Canada (Chairman, Earth Council)
Kazuo Takahashi, Japan (Director, International Development Research Institute)
Wilfried Thalwitz, Germany (Former Senior Vice President, World Bank)
José Israel Vargas, Brazil (Former Minister for Science and Technology, and President, Third World Academy of Sciences, Brazil)

Senior advisors

The Commission established a panel of Senior Advisors in March 1999. The panel's mission was to:

● Review documents being provided to the Commission.

● Identify areas they believe the Commission should consider priorities.

The panel members, all authorities on water resource management, are listed below.

Mohamed Ait-Kadi, President, General Council of Agricultural Development, Morocco
Arthur Askew, Director, Hydrology and Water Resources Department, World Meteorological Organization
John Briscoe, Senior Water Advisor, World Bank
Roger de Loose, General Coordinator, Poverty and Hunger Alleviation Task Force, Rotary International
Bert Diphoorn, Senior Water Advisor, Ministry of Foreign Affairs, The Netherlands
Farouk El-Baz, Director, Center for Remote Sensing, Boston University

Walter Falcon, Director, Institute for International Studies, Stanford University

Malin Falkenmark, Senior Scientist, Stockholm International Water Institute

Gourisankar Ghosh, Chief, Water, Environment and Sanitation Department, United Nations Children's Fund

Henry J. Hatch, Chief Executive Officer, American Society of Civil Engineers

Richard Helmer, Director, Division of Operational Support in Environmental Health, World Health Organization

Torkil Jönch-Clausen, Chairman, Technical Advisory Committee, Global Water Partnership

Guy Le Moigne, Former Executive Director, World Water Council

Roberto Lenton, Director, Sustainable Energy and Development Division, United Nations Development Programme

Richard Meganck, Director, Unit of Sustainable Development and Environment, Organization of American States

Sandra Postel, Director, Global Water Policy Project

Aly Shady, Senior Policy Advisor, Canadian International Development Agency

Motoyuki Suzuki, Vice Rector, United Nations University

Andras Szöllosi-Nagy, Director, Division of Water Sciences, United Nations Educational, Scientific, and Cultural Organization

Pierre-Frederic Tenière-Buchot, Senior Water Policy Advisor, United Nations Environment Programme

Appendix

vision mana

Vision Management Committee

Aly Shady (chair), Vice President, World Water Council, Egypt

Mohamed Ait-Kadi, Governor, World Water Council, Morocco

Jamil Al Alawi, Executive Director, World Water Council, Bahrain

William J. Cosgrove, Director, Vision Management Unit, ex officio, Canada

Rene Coulomb, Vice President, World Water Council, France

Bert Diphoorn, Ministry of Foreign Affairs, The Netherlands

Torkil Jönch-Clausen, Global Water Partnership, observer, Denmark.

Raymond Lafitte, Governor, World Water Council, France

John Pigram, Governor, World Water Council, Australia

Andras Szollosi-Nagy, Governor, World Water Council, Hungary

Vision Management Unit and Commission Secretariat

The implementation of Vision activities started with the establishment of the Vision Management Unit at the United Nations Educational, Scientific, and Cultural Organization in July 1998.

Director: William J. Cosgrove , Canada

Deputy Director: Frank R. Rijsberman, The Netherlands

Anne Baer, External Relations Consultant, France (September–December 1998)

Bozena Blix, Project Officer, Croatia

Malia Bouayad-Agha, Gender Coordinator, Algeria

Bongiwe Cele, Network Officer, South Africa

Subhrendu Gangopadhyay, Associate Expert, India

Constance Hunt, Senior Water Resources Professional, United States (April–September 1999)

Ariana Morris, Administrative Assistant, United Kingdom

Toshio Okazumi, River Basin Expert, Japan (October 1999–April 2000)

Ruud van der Helm, Network Officer, The Netherlands (April–December 1999)

Scenario Development Panel

Chairman: Ismail Serageldin, Egypt (Chairman, World Water Commission)

Co-Chairman: Frank R. Rijsberman, The Netherlands (World Water Vision Unit, Paris)

Secretary: Gilberto Gallopin, Argentina (Stockholm Environment Institute, Sweden)

Members

Jacob Adesida, Nigeria (United Nations Development Programme, Abidjan)

Joe Alcamo, United States (University of Kassel, Germany)

Nadezhda Gaponenko, Russia (Russian Academy of Sciences)

Peter Gleick, United States (Pacific Development Institute)

Stela Goldenstein, Brazil (Former Environment Secretary, São Paulo State)

Allen Hammond, United States (World Resources Institute)

Mark Rosegrant, United States (International Food Policy Research Institute)

David Seckler, United States (Director, International Water Management Institute, Sri Lanka)

Jill Slinger, South Africa (Council for Scientific and Industrial Research)

Sree Sreenath, India (Case Western Reserve University, United States)

Igor Shiklomanov, Russia (State Hydrology Institute)

Ken Strzepek, United States (University of Colorado)

Isabel Valencia, Venezuela

Rusong Wang, China (Chinese Academy of Sciences)

gement

Energy Panel

Chairman: Jamil Al-Alawi, Bahrain (Executive Director, World Water Council)

Boris Berkovsky, Russia (Head, Energy Division, United Nations Educational, Scientific, and Cultural Organization)

Ramesh Bhatia, India (Resources and Environment Group)

Michael Jefferson, United Kingdom (Director, Studies and Policy Development, World Energy Council)

Michael Klein, United Kingdom (Chief Economist, Shell International Limited)

Thierry Vandal, Canada (Vice President, Strategic Planning, Hydro-Quebec)

Information and Communication Technology Panel

Chairman: Iqbal Z. Quadir, Bangladesh (Director, GrameenPhone)

Michael B. Abbot, United Kingdom (International Institute for Infrastructural, Hydraulic, and Environmental Engineering–Delft)

Gunter Dueck, Germany (Distinguished Engineer, IBM)

Farouk El-Baz, Egypt (Director, Center for Remote Sensing, United States)

Hyunh Ngoc Phien, Vietnam (Computer Science and Information Management Program, School of Advanced Technology, Asian Institute of Technology)

Kuniyoshi Takeuchi, Japan (Department of Civil and Environmental Engineering, Yamanashi University)

Biotechnology Panel

Chairman: M.S. Swaminathan, India (M.S. Swaminathan Research Foundation)

Co-chairman: Ismail Seragaldin, Egypt (Vice President, World Bank, and Chairman, Consultative Group for International Agricultural Research)

Lisa Alvarez Cohen, United States (Associate Professor, Civil and Environmental Engineering, University of California at Berkeley)

Usha Barwale, India (Life Sciences Research Centre)

P.C. Kesavan, India (Homi-Bhabha Chair, M.S. Swaminathan Research Foundation)

Sudha Nair, India (Principal Scientist, M.S. Swaminathan Research Foundation)

Ajay K. Parida, India (Principal Scientist, M.S. Swaminathan Research Foundation)

C.S. Prakash, India (Centre for Plant Biotech Research)

Hanspeter Schelling, Switzerland (Novartis International AG)

Dillip Shah, India (Research and Development Director for India)

Institutions, Society, and the Economy Panel

Chairwoman: Margaret Catley-Carlson, Canada (International Consultant; Former President, Canadian International Development Agency and Population Council)

Nat Amartiefo, Ghana (Former Mayor, Accra, Ghana)

Jerry Delli Priscolli, United States (Institute of Water Resources, U.S. Corps of Engineers)

Chuck Howe, United States (Professor of Economics, University of Colorado)

Pierre-Marc Johnson, Canada (Environmental Lawyer, Former Prime Minister of Québec, member of Club of Lisbon)

Hideaki Oda, Japan (Former Director-General of River Bureau, Ministry of Construction)

Lilian Saade, Mexico (International Institute for Infrastructural, Hydraulic, and Environmental Engineering)

R. M. Saleth, India (Associate Professor, Institute of Economic Growth)

S.K. Sharma, India (Senior Advisor, Development Alternatives)

vision mana

Gender Advisory Committee

Malia Bouayad-Agha, Algeria (Gender Coordinator, World Water Vision Unit)

Mahnaz Afkhami, Iran (President, Women's Learning Partnership for Rights, Development, and Peace)

Ingvar Andersson, Sweden (Senior Freshwater Advisor, Water Programme, Sustainable Energy and Environment Division, United Nations Development Programme)

Kusum Athukorala, Sri Lanka (Global Water Partnership)

Joke Blom, The Netherlands (Director, International Information Centre and Archives for the Women's Movement)

Aggrey Chemonges, Kenya (Regional Consultant for Africa, United Nations Development Fund for Women)

Rekha Dayal, India (Director, Mallika Consultants)

Fatoumata Diallo, Burkina Faso (Green Cross International)

Christina Espinosa, Peru (Global Facilitator, World Conservation Union)

Jennifer Francis, Malaysia (Programme Officer, IRC International Water and Sanitation Centre)

Teckie Ghebre-Medhin, Eritrea (Economic Empowerment Senior Advisor, United Nations Development Fund for Women)

Nighisty Ghezae, Sweden (Global Water Partnership)

Bruce Gross, United States (Consultant, Water and Sanitation Programme, World Bank)

Danielle Hirsch, The Netherlands (Assistant Programme Specialist, Forest and Water, Both ENDS)

Maliha Hussein, Pakistan (South Asia Technical Advisory Committee of the Global Water Partnership National Coordinator)

Margaret Jenkins, Canada (Assistant Programme Specialist, Economic Empowerment Programme, United Nations Development Fund for Women)

Annelie Joki-Hubach, The Netherlands (Consultant, IRC International Water and Sanitation Center)

Gerd Johnsson, Sweden (Councellor, Ministry for Foreign Affairs—Sweden)

Tabeth Matiza-Chiuta, Zimbabwe (World Conservation Union)

Ruth Meinzen-Dick, United States (Senior Research Fellow, International Food Policy Research Institute)

Lailun Nahar Ekram, Bangladesh (Global Water Partnership)

Breda Pavlic, Slovenia (Director, UNESCO Unit for the Status of Women and Gender Equality)

Lin Pugh, Australia (Manager, Knowledge Sharing Program, International Information Centre and Archives for the Women's Movement)

Amreeta Regmi, Nepal (Regional Consultant for South Asia, United Nations Development Fund for Women)

Gabriella Richardson, Sweden (Social Policy and Gender Officer, World Conservation Union)

Lydia Ruprecht, Canada (Assistant Programme Specialist, UNESCO Unit for the Status of Women and Gender Equality)

Cecilia Tortajada, Mexico (Vice President, Third World Centre for Water Management)

Ruud van der Helm, The Netherlands (Youth Coordinator, World Water Vision Unit)

Meike van Ginneken, The Netherlands (Global Water Partnership)

Barbara van Koppen, The Netherlands (Coordinator, Gender and Water Program, International Water Management Institute)

Frank van Steenbergen, The Netherlands (Global Water Partnership, Framework for Action Unit)

Christine van Wijk, The Netherlands (Senior Programme Officer, IRC International Water and Sanitation Centre)

Wendy Wakeman, United States (Community Development Specialist, World Bank)

Paul Wolvekamp, The Netherlands (Coordinator, Forest and Water, Both ENDS)

gement

Background papers and modelling

Nancy Contreras, Research Associate, Third World Centre for Water Management, Mexico

Gordon Conway, President, Rockefeller Foundation, United States

Peter Gleick, President, Pacific Development Institute, United States

Kenneth Strzepek, Professor, University of Colorado/Stockholm Environmental Institute, United States

Center for Environmental Systems Research, University of Kassel, Germany

International Food Policy Research Institute, United States

International Water Management Institute, Sri Lanka

State Hydrological Institute, Russia

Stockholm Environmental Institute, Sweden

Appendix

Sectors

Water for People (Vision 21)
Water Supply and Sanitation Collaborative Council, Switzerland

Water for Food
CEMAGREF, France
DVWK, Germany
Food and Agriculture Organization/International Programme for Technology and Research in Irrigation and Drainage, Italy
HR Wallingford, United Kingdom
International Commission on Irrigation and Drainage, India
International Food Policy Research Institute, United States
International Institute for Land Reclamation and Improvement, The Netherlands
International Water Management Institute, Sri Lanka
McGill University, Brace Centre for Water Resources Management, Canada
Wageningen Agricultural University, The Netherlands
World Bank, United States

Water and Nature
World Conservation Union, Montreal Office, Canada

Water in Rivers
Center for Research on River Basin Administration, Analysis and Management, Delft University of Technology, The Netherlands
International Association for Hydraulic Research, The Netherlands
International Network of River Basin Organizations, France
Japanese Ministry of Construction, Japan

Water and Sovereignty
Green Cross International, Switzerland

Interbasin Water Transfer
United Nations Educational, Scientific, and Cultural Organization–International Hydrological Programme, France

Water for Tourism and Recreation
John Pigram, Center for Water Policy Research, University of New England, Australia

Water, Education, and Training
United Nations Educational, Scientific, and Cultural Organization—International Hydrological Programme, France

Regions

Africa Coordination
African Development Bank, Côte d'Ivoire

Southern Africa
Global Water Partnership–Southern Africa Technical Advisory Committee, Zimbabwe

West Africa
Global Water Partnership–West Africa Technical Advisory Committee, Burkina Faso

Nile Basin
Ministry of Public Works and Water Resources, Egypt
Nile Basin Initiative, Uganda

Arab countries
Economic and Social Commission for Africa, Ethiopia
United Nations Educational, Scientific, and Cultural Organization, Regional Office for Science and Technology for the Arab States, Egypt
United Nations Environment Programme, Kenya
World Water Council, France

Mediterranean
Global Water Partnership–Mediterranean Technical Advisory Committee, France
Plan Bleu (Blue Plan), France

Rhine Basin
Ministry of Transport, Public Works and Water Resources Management, The Netherlands

Central and Eastern Europe
Global Water Partnership–Central and Eastern Europe Technical Advisory Committee, Hungary

Russia
Russian Academy of Sciences, Russia

Aral Sea Basin
United Nations Educational, Scientific, and Cultural Organization–International Hydrological Programme, France

South Asia
Global Water Partnership–South Asia Technical Advisory Committee, India

Southeast Asia
Global Water Partnership–Southeast Asia Technical Advisory Committee, The Philippines

China
Chinese Academy of Sciences, China

Australia and New Zealand
Center for Water Policy Research, University of New England, Australia

Americas Coordination
Global Water Partnership–South America Technical Advisory Committee, Chile
Organization of American States, United States

South America
Global Water Partnership–South America Technical Advisory Committee, Chile

Central America and the Caribbean
Cathalac, Water Center for the Humid Tropics of Latin America and the Caribbean, Panama

North America
McGill University, Brace Centre for Water Resources Management, Canada
National Commission for Water, Mexico
The Nature Conservancy, United States
Organization of American States, United States
Water Environment Federation, United States

Gender
Both ENDS (Environment and Development Service for NGOs), The Netherlands
International Information Centre and Archives for the Women Movement, The Netherlands
International Water Management Institute, Sri Lanka
IRC International Water and Sanitation Centre, The Netherlands
United Nations Development Fund for Women, United States

Youth
Globetree Foundation, Sweden
The Hague International Model United Nations, The Netherlands
Junior Chamber International, United States

meetings ar

August 1998

Announcement of the Formation of the World Commission on Water for the 21st Century
Stockholm, Sweden
August 11

September 1998

First Scenario Development Panel Meeting
Washington, D.C.
September 24–25

October 1998

Water for Food Preparatory Meeting
Rabat, Morocco
October 27–28

November 1998

Global Water Partnership–Technical Advisory Committee Meeting
Warsaw, Poland
November 8–9

Scenario Development Panel Meeting
Washington, D.C.
November 9–10

Water and Nature Preparatory Meeting
Dakar, Senegal
November 9–13

Water for People Preparatory Meeting
Abidjan, Côte d'Ivoire
November 16–20

Thematic Panel on Energy
Paris, France
November 20

January 1999

Donor Meeting
Paris, France
January 26

Scoping Meeting for Southern Africa
Harare, Zimbabwe
January 28–29

Scoping Meeting for West Africa
Ouagadougou, Burkina Faso
January 28–29

February 1999

Thematic Panel on Biotechnology
Chennai, India
February 4–5

Thematic Panel on Information and Communication Technology
Paris, France
February 5

Scoping Meeting for South Asia
New Delhi, India
February 13–14

Thematic Panel on Institutions, Society, and the Economy
Paris, France
February 18–19

March 1999

Scoping Meeting for South America
Cali, Colombia
March 2–3

Nile 2000
Cairo, Egypt
March 15–18

Global Water Partnership–Technical Advisory Committee Meeting in Cairo
Cairo, Egypt
March 19

Board Meeting of the World Water Council
Cairo, Egypt
March 20–21

Extended Vision Team Meeting with Senior Advisors on World Water Day
Cairo, Egypt
March 22

First Meeting of the World Commission on Water for the 21st Century
Cairo, Egypt
March 23

Discussion of Social Charter for Water
Paris, France
March 25

Vision Workshop at the Third Dialogue on Water Management
Panama, Panama
March 25–26

April 1999

Vision Workshop on Water and Nature—Freshwater Ecosystem Management and Social Security
Harare, Zimbabwe
April 13–15

China Regional Scoping Meeting
Shanghai, China
April 15–16

Vision Consultation at the European Geophysical Society Meeting
The Hague, the Netherlands
April 19–23

Meeting of the Knowledge Synthesis Group for Water Supply and Sanitation (Vision 21)
Wageningen, the Netherlands
April 20–22

Technical Consultation for Aral Sea Basin Regional Vision
Tashkent, Uzbekistan
April 26

International Workshop on Interbasin Water Transfer
Paris, France
April 26–27

Global Water Partnership–South Asia Technical Advisory Committee: Mapping through NGO-GO Interaction Meeting for India
Ahmedabad, India
April 26–27

Water for Food: International Commission on Irrigation and Drainage–Coordinated Meeting on East Asia
Shanghai, China
April 26–28

Presentation of the Vision Project at Scientific Committee on Water Research Meeting of the International Council for Science
Paris, France
April 27

May 1999

Global Water Partnership–Technical Advisory Committee Meeting in Budapest
Budapest, Hungary
May 3–7

Preparation of the First Draft of Water for People Sectoral Consultation (Vision 21)
London, England
May 4–7 (with an extension to May 15 for the completion group)

Sub-Regional Expert Consultation on Water for Food: Food and Agriculture Organization–Coordinated Meeting on West Africa
Accra, Ghana
May 6–7

Global Water Partnership–South Asia Technical Advisory Committee: Sri Lankan Country Vision Meeting
Colombo, Sri Lanka
May 6–7

Presentation of Vision Project and Discussion of Vision for Arab Countries at Water for Sustainable Growth Conference
Amman, Jordan
May 8–11

Water for Food and Rural Development Sectoral Consultation for Europe
Bratislava, Slovak Republic
May 10–11

Regional Scoping Meeting for Global Water Partnership–Southeast Asia Technical Advisory Committee
Manila, the Philippines
May 13–14

Global Water Partnership–South Asia Technical Advisory Committee: India Country Vision Meeting
New Delhi, India
May 16–17

Water for Food and Rural Development Consultation for East Asia
Kuala Lumpur, Malaysia
May 17–19

Presentation of the Vision Project and Discussion of the Lake Biwa Regional Vision at the Eighth International Conference on the Conservation and Management of Lakes
Copenhagen, Denmark
May 17–21

Global Water Partnership–South Asia Technical Advisory Committee: Bangladesh Country Vision Meeting
Dhaka, Bangladesh
May 20–21

Global Water Partnership–South Asia Technical Advisory Committee: Pakistan Country Vision Meeting
Lahore, Pakistan
May 24–25

Presentation of the Vision Project at the Africa Water Resources Policy Conference
Nairobi, Kenya
May 24–27

Sub-Regional Expert Consultation on Water for Food: Food and Agriculture Organization–Coordinated Meeting on East and Southern Africa
Harare, Zimbabwe
May 26–27

Water for Food: CEMAGREF/HR Wallingford–Coordinated Meeting for Middle East and North Africa
Bari, Italy
May 27–29

Global Water Partnership–South Asia Technical Advisory Committee: Mapping Meeting for Nepal
Kathmandu, Nepal
May 28

Global Water Partnership–South Asia Technical Advisory Committee: Nepal Country Vision Meeting
Kathmandu, Nepal
May 29–30

Vision Report Drafting Team Meeting
Paris, France
May 31–June 4

June 1999

Water for Food and Rural Development Sectoral Consultation for South Asia
New Delhi, India
June 1–3

Discussion of the Vision Project at The Learning Society and the Water-Environment International Symposium
Paris, France
June 2–4

Presentation of the Vision Project at Water 99: Third Annual International Water Conference
Dundee, United Kingdom
June 6–10

Vision Workshop on Water and Nature: Freshwater Ecosystem Management and Economic Security
Bangkok, Thailand
June 9–11

Presentation and Discussion of Global Water Partnership–Mediterranean Technical Advisory Committee Regional Vision at Technical Advisory Committee Meeting in Budapest
Budapest, Hungary
June 9–10

Women and Water: Sisterhood Is Global Institute Networking and Brainstorming Meeting on Women's Participation in the Vision Process
Washington, D.C.
June 10–12

National Visions for Central and Eastern Europe Presented at Technical Advisory Committee Meeting in Budapest
Budapest, Hungary
June 11–12

Scenario Drafting Team Meeting
Paris, France
June 14–18

Discussion of Vision Project and the Water for Food Sectoral Vision for the Americas at Ministerial Meeting
Montevideo, Uruguay
June 15–18

Presentation of the Vision Project and Discussion of Freshwater Issues at the United Nations Environment and Development (UNED-UK)–sponsored Building Partnerships for Sustainable Development Conference
London, United Kingdom
June 16

Vision Workshop on Water and Nature: Freshwater Ecosystem Management and Environmental Security
San Jose, Costa Rica
June 20–22

National Consultation Meeting on Water Sector Mapping and Vision
Kuala Lumpur, Malaysia
June 28

Scenario Development Panel Meeting
Paris, France
June 28–29

South Asia Regional Conference on South Asia Vision
Colombo, Sri Lanka
June 28–29

Canada Vision Consultation
Montreal, Canada
June 28–29

Second Reference Group Meeting for Global Water Partnership–Southern Africa Technical Advisory Committee
Pretoria, South Africa
June 30

Mapping Meeting for Global Water Partnership–South Asia Technical Advisory Committee
Colombo, Sri Lanka
June 30

Water for Food Consultations for the Americas
Montreal, Canada
June 30–July 2

July 1999

Consultation on a Regional Water Vision for the Danube Basin
Hungary, Budapest
July 1

First Regional Stakeholder Meeting for Global Water Partnership–Southern Africa Technical Advisory Committee
Pretoria, South Africa
July 1–2

Global Water Partnership–Mediterranean Technical Advisory Committee Vision Presentation for the Mediterranean Commission for Sustainable Development
Rome, Italy
July 1–3

Presentation of the Vision Project at the African International Environmental Protection Symposium (AIPES 99)
Pietermaritzburg, South Africa
July 4

Discussion of Global Water Partnership–Mediterranean Technical Advisory Committee Regional Scenarios at the Committee's General Assembly Meeting
Valette, Malta
July 5–7

Appendix

Vision Report Drafting Team Meeting
Paris, France
July 5–9

Vision for Rainwater Catchment Systems in the 21st Century at the Second Brazilian Rainwater Catchment Symposium
Petrolina, Brazil
July 6–9

Presentation of the Vision Project and Australia's Draft Vision at Water 99 Joint Congress: 25th Hydrology and Water Resources Symposium
Brisbane, Australia
July 7

Preliminary Meeting for Water in Rivers Sectoral Vision
Tokyo, Japan
July 7–8

Meeting for Global Water Partnership–West Africa Technical Advisory Committee
Ouadagoudou, Burkina Faso
July 17–18

August 1999

Water for Food and Rural Development Sectoral Consultation for Central Asian Republics
Tashkent, Uzbekistan
August 3–6

Arab Countries Vision Consultation
Marseilles, France
August 4–5

Global Water Partnership–Technical Advisory Committee Meeting in Stockholm
Stockholm, Sweden
August 7–8

Second Meeting of the World Commission on Water for the 21st Century
Stockholm, Sweden
August 9

Workshop on Vision-in-Progress during Stockholm Water Symposium
Stockholm, Sweden
August 10

Zimbabwe National Consultation for Global Water Partnership–Southern Africa Technical Advisory Committee
Harare, Zimbabwe
August 24

Latin America Regional Consultation for Vision 21 (Water for People)
Quito, Ecuador
August 25–27

Lesotho National Consultation for Global Water Partnership–Southern Africa Technical Advisory Committee
Meserv, Lesotho
August 31

September 1999

Namibia National Consultation for Global Water Partnership–Southern Africa Technical Advisory Committee
Windhoek, Namibia
September 2

Malawi National Consultation for Global Water Partnership–Southern Africa Technical Advisory Committee
Lilongwe, Malawi
September 8

Central and Eastern European Regional Vision Consultation
Vilnius, Lithuania
September 10–11

Presentation of the Water for Food Vision at the 17th International Commission on Irrigation and Drainage Conference on Water for Agriculture in the Next Millennium
Granada, Spain
September 11–19

Africa Regional Water for People Sectoral Consultation (Vision 21)
Dakar, Senegal
September 13–17

Presentation of the Vision Project at the 11th Asia Pacific and 2nd Commonwealth Congress of Environmental Journalists
Dhaka, Bangladesh
September 13–17

Botswana National Consultation for Global Water Partnership–Southern Africa Technical Advisory Committee
Gaberone, Botswana
September 14

Brainstorming Meeting for a French Vision
Paris, France
September 15

South Africa National Consultation for Global Water Partnership–Southern Africa Technical Advisory Committee
Pretoria, South Africa
September 16

Ministerial Conference Preparatory Meeting
The Hague, The Netherlands
September 20–21

From Vision to Action: India Regional Vision and Framework for Action Workshop
New Delhi, India
September 20–21

Swaziland National Consultation for Global Water Partnership–Southern Africa Technical Advisory Committee
Lobamba, Swaziland
September 21

Presentation of the Vision Project at the Integrated Drought Management: Lessons for Sub-Saharan Africa Conference
Pretoria, South Africa
September 22

Mozambique National Consultation for Global Water Partnership–Southern Africa Technical Advisory Committee
Maputo, Mozambique
September 23

Asia Regional Consultation for Vision 21 (Water for People)
Bangkok, Thailand
September 24–25

Small Island Countries Regional Consultation for Vision 21 (Water for People)
Trinidad
September 29–30

Tanzania National Consultation for Global Water Partnership–Southern Africa Technical Advisory Committee
Tanzania
September 30

October 1999

World Water Vision Modellers Meeting
Colombo, Sri Lanka
October 1–2

Vision Explorer Presentation at the Water Information Summit
Fort Lauderdale, Florida
October 3–6

Zambia National Consultation for Global Water Partnership–Southern Africa Technical Advisory Committee
Lunited stateska, Zambia
October 6

First Sri Lanka Framework for Action Consultation
Colombo, Sri Lanka
October 8

Angola National Consultation for Global Water Partnership–Southern Africa Technical Advisory Committee
Luanda, Angola
October 13

Estonia National Consultation for Global Water Partnership–Central and Eastern Europe Technical Advisory Committee
Tallin, Estonia
October 15

Lithuania National Consultation for Global Water Partnership–Central and Eastern Europe Technical Advisory Committee
Vilnius, Lithuania
October 15

Pakistan Framework for Action Consultation
Islamabad, Pakistan
October 17

Presentation of First Draft of Mediterranean Vision, Mapping, and Action Strategies at the Euro-Mediterranean Water Conference
Turin, Italy
October 18–19

Writing Meeting for Southern Africa Regional Vision
Harare, Zimbabwe
October 18–22

Report on Status of the Vision Project at the Foundation for Water Research's Conference on Working Together to Meet the World's Water Needs
Birmingham, United Kingdom
October 19

Meeting of National Groups for Aral Sea Vision
Tashkent, Uzbekistan
October 22

Bulgaria National Consultation for Global Water Partnership–Central and Eastern Europe Technical Advisory Committee
Sofia, Bulgaria
October 25–26

Water and Nature Vision Drafting Meeting
Gland, Switzerland
October 26

Presentation of First Draft of Mediterranean Vision, Mapping, and Action Strategies at Meeting of Barcelona Convention Signatories
Barcelona, Spain
October 27–30

Central and Eastern European Regional Vision Consultation
Ljubljana, Slovenia
October 30

November 1999

Water in Rivers Sectoral Consultation
Tokyo, Japan
November 1–3

Second Regional Stakeholder Meeting for Global Water Partnership–Southern Africa Technical Advisory Committee
Gaberone, Botswana
November 8–9

United States Water Vision Consultation
Arlington, Virginia
November 9–10

Third Reference Group Meeting for Global Water Partnership–Southern Africa Technical Advisory Committee
Gaborone, Botswana
November 10

Scenario Development Panel Meeting
Paris, France
November 11–12

Bangladesh National Vision Consultation on the Framework for Action, Youth, and Gender
Dhaka, Bangladesh
November 13–15

North America Consultation
Miami, Florida
November 15–16

Global Consultation for Vision 21 (Water for People)
Gujarat, India
November 15–16

Presentation of the Vision Project at Investing in the Future of the Global Water Industry Conference
London, United Kingdom
November 18–19

NGO Consultation on India Water Vision
November 27–29
Mumbai, India
Senior Advisors Meeting
The Hague, the Netherlands
November 28

Commission Meeting
The Hague, The Netherlands
November 28–30

December 1999

World Water Forum Presentation Coordinating Meeting
The Hague, The Netherlands
December 1

South America Regional Technical Advisory Committee
Meeting
Lima, Peru
December 6–8

Presentation of the Vision Project at the Modeling the
Dynamics of Natural, Agricultural, Hydrological, Tourism, and
Socio-Economic Systems Conference (MODSIM 99)
Hamilton, New Zealand
December 6–9

South Asia Regional Conference on South Asia Vision and
Framework for Action
Dkaka, Bangladesh
December 6–9

India Framework for Action Consultation
Chennai, India
December 13–14

PODIUM Review Workshop
New Delhi, India
December 14-15

National Consultation Meeting on Vision
Kuala Lumpur, Malaysia
December 18

Drafting Team Meeting for the Western Africa Regional Vision
Accra, Ghana
December 18–20

Framework for Action and Technical Advisory Committee
Meeting
London, United Kingdom
December 20

January 2000

Social Charter for Water Advisory Group Meeting
Paris, France
January 14

Southeast Asia Technical Advisory Committee Meeting
Manila, The Philippines
January 19–21

Global Water Partnership–Technical Advisory Committee
Meeting
Manila, The Philippines
January 20

International Preparatory Committee Meeting for Ministerial
Conference
Amsterdam, The Netherlands
January 30–February 1

February 2000

Global Water Partnership, Financial Support Group
Amsterdam, The Netherlands
February 2

Forum International Steering Committee
Cairo, Egypt
February 4

Africa-wide Stakeholder Consultation
Abidjan, Côte d'Ivoire, or Addis Ababa, Ethiopia
February 8–9

National Consultation Meeting on Vision to Action
Kuala Lumpur, Malaysia
February 18

March 2000

Second World Water Forum
The Hague, The Netherlands
March 17–22

Appendix

All background documents are available on the CD-ROM that accompanies this book.

Secretariat documents

Thematic Panel Reports, World Water Vision Unit, November 1998–March 1999.

World Water Scenarios: Analysis, Frank R. Rijsberman, ed., Forthcoming publication from Earthscan, London.

Mainstreaming Gender in Water Resources Management: Why and How: Background Paper for the World Water Vision Process, N. Maharaj, ed., October 1999.

Regional vision documents

Africa
The Africa Water Vision for 2025: Equitable & Sustainable Use of Water for Socioeconomic Development, African Caucus, December 1999.

West Africa
West Africa Water Vision, Global Water Partnership–West Africa Technical Advisory Committee, December 1999.

Southern Africa
Southern Africa Vision for Water, Life and the Environment in the 21st Century and Strategic Framework for Action Statement, Global Water Partnership–Southern Africa Technical Advisory Committee, November 1998.

Nile Basin
The Vision for Water in the 21st Century for the Countries of the Nile River Basin, A. Shady, ed., March 1999.

Arab countries
Water Vision for the Arab Countries towards the Year 2025. K.F. Saad, November 1999.

Mediterranean
Mediterranean Vision on Water, Population and the Environment for the XXIst Century, J. Margat and D. Vallee, October 1999.

Rhine Basin
Visions for the Rhine, Rhine Basin Vision Project Group, October 1999.

Central and Eastern Europe
A Vision of Water Resources Management in Central and Eastern Europe, Global Water Partnership–Central and Eastern Europe Technical Advisory Committee, August 1999.

Water Management Mapping Report for the Danube Sub-region Countries of Eastern and Central Europe: Bulgaria, Czech Republic, Hungary, Romania, Slovakia and Slovenia, Global Water Partnership–Central and Eastern Europe Technical Advisory Committee, May 1999.

Water Resources Management Mapping and Vision for the Baltic Sub-region of Eastern and Central Europe: Estonia, Latvia, Lithuania and Poland, M. Nawalany, June 1999.

Russia
Russian Water Vision: Scenarios of Russian Water Sector Development, N. Gaponenko, August 1999.

Aral Sea Basin
Water-related Aral Sea Basin Vision for the Year 2025, United Nations Educational, Scientific, and Cultural Organization–International Hydrological Programme, October 1999.

South Asia
South Asia Regional Water Vision 2025, Global Water Partnership–South Asia Technical Advisory Committee, July 1999.

China
China Vision, R. Wang, Z. Ouyang, H. Ren, and Q. Min, November 1999.

Australia and New Zealand
A Vision for Australia's Water Resources 2025, J. Pigram and B. Hooper, November 1999.

Americas
The Vision on Water, Life and the Environment in the 21st Century: The Americas, Inter-American Water Resources Network, December 1999.

documents

South America
South America Regional Vision and Framework for Action, Global Water Partnership–South America Technical Advisory Committee, August 1999.

Central America and Caribbean
Vision on Water, Life and the Environment for the 21st Century: Regional Visions: Central America and the Caribbean, Water Center for the Humid Tropics of Latin America and the Caribbean, August 1999.

North America
Canadian Roundtable on a Vision for Water, Life and the Environment for the 21st Century, C. Madramootoo, June 1999.

Vision on Water, Life and the Environment for the 21st Century: Regional Consultations: North America, Mexican National Commission for Water, December 1999.

Sector vision documents

Water for People
Vision 21: Water for People: A Shared Vision for Water Supply, Sanitation and Hygiene and a Framework for Mobilisation of Action, Water Supply and Sanitation Collaborative Council, December 1999.

Urban Water and Sanitation Systems, T. Milburn, November 1999.

Water and Nature
Freshwater and Related Ecosystems—The Source of Life and the Responsibility of All: A World Water Vision for Sustainable Management of Water Resources in the 21st Century, World Conservation Union, October 1999.

Water and Nature Discussion Papers
Freshwater Ecosystems, Conflict Management & Economic Security, T. Swanson and C. Doble, May 1999.

Freshwater Ecosystems Management & Environmental Security, M.P. McCartney, M.C. Acreman, and G. Bergkamp, June 1999.

Freshwater Ecosystems Management & Social Security: A Discussion Paper for IUCN, J. Soussan, N. Emmel, and C. Howorth, March 1999.

Water for Food
A Vision of Water for Food and Rural Development, P. van Hofwegen and M. Svendsen, November 1999.

Water in Rivers
Report on Sector Consultation "Water in Rivers", H. Oda, November 1999.

Water in Rivers: Flooding, R. White, September 1999.

Contribution to the World Water Vision, International Network of Basin Organizations, November 1999.

Recommendations and Guidelines on Sustainable River Basin Management: Workshop Report of "International Workshop on River Basin Management", Center for Research on River Basin Administration, Analysis and Management, Delft University of Technology, October 1999.

Sovereignty
National Sovereignty and International Water Courses, Green Cross International, November 1999.

Interbasin Water Transfer
Interbasin Water Transfer, United Nations Educational, Scientific, and Cultural Organization–International Hydrological Programme, April 1999.

Water for Tourism and Recreation
A Vision for Water and Tourism—2025, J. Pigram, November 1999.

Water, Education, and Training
Water, Education and Training, United Nations Educational, Scientific, and Cultural Organization–International Hydrological Programme, October 1999.

Glossary

aquifer a layer of earth or rock containing groundwater.

blue water renewable water resources—the portion of rainfall that enters into streams and recharges groundwater.

consultations process through which more than 40 groups around the world developed sector and regional visions and commented on the evolving World Water Vision.

criticality ratio ratio of water withdrawals to total renewable water resources, preferably on a basin scale.

current basin use ratio of consumptive use in a basin to the primary water supply. When this factor is low say, 30% water could be saved and put to more productive use. When it is high—say, 70%—increasing water consumption is likely to be difficult and undesirable from a perspective of leaving sufficient water in nature and for the environment.

dams, large defined by the International Commission on Large Dams as having a height over 15 metres.

——, **International Commission on** established by the World Conservation Union and the World Bank to carry out a balanced analysis of all the costs and benefits of large dams—and propose criteria to evaluate the social, economic, and environmental desirability of proposed dam projects. Will deliver its report by mid-2000.

drivers the key factors, trends, or processes that influence a situation, focal issue, or decision, propel the system forward, and determine a scenario's outcome.

Falkenmark indicator renewable water resources per capita per year—usually held to show that water stress begins when the indicator is below 1,700 cubic metres a year and becomes severe when it falls below 1,000 cubic metres a year.

fossil water groundwater that has accumulated over a long period—often in previous geological periods—and is not or barely recharged. Not a renewable resource.

Framework for Action programme of the Global Water Partnership to develop a framework of actions at the regional level that would achieve the World Water Vision objectives.

full-cost pricing users pay the full cost of obtaining, collecting, treating, and distributing water, as well as collecting, treating, and disposing of wastewater.

gender mainstreaming incorporation of gender perspectives into water resource management strategies requires attention to the complex relationship between productive and domestic uses of water resources, to the importance of participation in decisionmaking for all (women and men), and to the equitable distribution of benefits from improved infrastructure and management systems for all (SIDA 1997).

Global Water Partnership an international network established in 1996, open to all organisations involved in water resource management, created in response to the need to promote integrated water resource management through activities at the field level.

green water soil water—the portion of rainfall that is stored in the soil and evaporates from it; used by ecosystems and as source for rainfed agriculture.

groundwater water contained in the saturated zone of a layer of earth or rock.

——, **recharge** amount of water—mostly rainfall—that percolates through soil and enters groundwater.

innovation change in technology or management that improves the productivity, efficiency, or effectiveness of water use; relates to improvements ranging from improved membrane technology that reduces the cost of desalination to institutional changes that improve farmers' control over water supply and thereby yields.

integrated water resource management philosophy that holds that water must be viewed from a holistic perspective, both in its natural state and in balancing competing demands on it—agricultural, industrial, domestic, and environmental. Management of water resources and services needs to reflect the interaction between these different demands, and so must be coordinated within and across sectors. If the many cross-cutting requirements are met, and if there can be horizontal and vertical integration within the management framework for water resources and services, a more equitable, efficient, and sustainable regime will emerge (Global Water Partnership, Framework for Action 1999).

irrigated area, harvested cropped area. For example, a 1-hectare plot that has two crops per year counts as 2 hectares.

Glossary

——, **net** physical area of irrigated agricultural land.

irrigation, deficit aims to increase productivity per unit of water with irrigation strategies that do not fully meet evaporative requirements.

——, **precision** aims to reduce nonbeneficial evaporation through more uniform application; includes drip irrigation, precision sprinklers, and level basins (laser levelling).

——, **supplemental** irrigation supplementing limited rainfed agriculture during critical periods in the growing season.

model a schematic description of a system, theory, or phenomenon that accounts for its known or inferred properties and may be used for further study of its characteristics.

——, **IMPACT:** an economic model developed by the International Food Policy Research Institute to analyse the supply of and demand for world food and consequences for world food trade (Rosegrant and Ringler 1999).

——, **PODIUM:** a water policy model developed by the International Water Management Institute to analyse the supply of and demand for water resources, with detailed analysis of the water for food and rural development at the national and global levels (IWMI 2000).

——, **WaterGAP:** a global model combining a hydrology component based on climate factors with a dynamic analysis of uses; relies on a 0.5 by 0.5 degree grid for analysis at the river basin level. Developed by the Centre for Environmental Systems Research at the University of Kassel (Alcamo and others 1999).

overextraction groundwater extraction that exceeds recharge and results in dropping groundwater tables.

potential basin use ratio of consumptive use in a river basin to the usable water supply. Where this is lower than current basin use there is scope for water resource development from a technical and economic perspective; does not indicate whether such development is socially or environmentally desirable.

primary water supply amount of water that can be diverted or pumped with current infrastructure.

productivity amount of products or services produced per unit of water consumed. At a fixed demand for products or services, increasing productivity means reducing the demand for water. Increasing productivity can be the result of technological as well as management improvements.

rainwater harvesting efforts to increase the amount of rainfall captured and stored for later use. Usually refers to small-scale, household or community-based efforts to increase the amount of rainfall that recharges groundwater or to capture runoff from fields or roofs in small storage structures such as tanks.

renewable water resources the portion of rainfall that enters into streams and recharges groundwater.

sanitation disposal of household and industrial wastewater, excreta, and so on.

scarcity, economic indicates that sufficient water resources are available to meet demand but that water supplies would need to be developed to do so, creating a financial and capacity problem when economic scarcity is high.

——, **physical** indicates that even with the highest feasible efficiency and productivity of water, there are insufficient resources to meet demand.

scenario story about the future with a logical plot and narrative governing the manner in which events unfold. A possible course of events leading to a resulting state of the world (or image of the future), not a forecast or projection.

sovereignty the right of national governments to manage and use water resources that originate in or pass through their national territory as they see fit. In international basins cooperation over shared management of water resources is of paramount importance. Increased cooperation would lead governments to voluntarily accept limitations on their sovereignty over water.

storage to retain flood water for later human use. Includes traditional means such as small tanks and large and small reservoirs, as well as storage in groundwater aquifers.

surface water water in streams, rivers, or lakes.

usable water supply the amount of renewable resources that can be used if all technically and economically feasible storage and diversion structures are built.

valuing ecosystem functions healthy ecosystems, both freshwater and terrestrial, provide many services from fish and wildlife production to flood control to recreation. More research into ecosystem functioning is needed to assess the values of the services provided.

vision a desirable future and the way to get there.

——, **global** global World Water Vision describes a desirable water future for 2025 for all uses and for the world as a whole as well as the key strategic actions required to achieve this future.

——, **plural** given that different stakeholders from various parts of the world have different backgrounds, experiences, and interests, a single World Water Vision that has the support of everybody is not likely to evolve except at the level of basic principles. There will be plural visions on what constitutes a desirable water future, but what counts is to achieve a widely shared agreement on urgent actions to move in the right direction. This agreement should involve a much larger section of the population than to date.

——, **regional** vision of a desirable water future for 2025 for all water uses in a specific region—such as South Asia, the Mediterranean, or Southern Africa. More than 15 regional Visions were developed as part of the World Water Vision exercise.

——, **sector** vision for a desirable water future at a global scale for a specific water subsector. Sector visions were developed through extensive consultations for Water for People (Vision 21), Water and Nature, Water for Food and Rural Development, and Water in Rivers. Special, more limited efforts were undertaken for Water and Tourism, a Social Charter, and Water Sovereignty.

virtual water water used to produce a good or service. For example, 1 kilogram of wheat contains at least 1,000 litres of virtual water.

Vision Management Unit unit of the World Water Council responsible for day-to-day management of the World Water Vision exercise. Housed in the Paris headquarters of the United Nations Educational, Scientific, and Cultural Organization.

water consumed water delivered to a use that is evaporated or incorporated into products and organisms, such that it becomes unavailable to other users.

water crisis the current widespread and chronic lack of access to safe and affordable drinking water and sanitation, the high incidence of water-related diseases, the destruction of wetlands, and the degradation of water quality in rivers and lakes.

watershed an area from which rainfall flows off through one particular watercourse. A large watershed is often composed of subwatersheds because each tributary of a main river has its own watershed.

water stress an indicator of insufficient water of satisfactory quality and quantity to meet human and environmental needs.

water subsidies government funds that cover part of the cost, directly or indirectly, of making water services available to users and disposing of wastewater.

water use the renewable resources withdrawn from surface and groundwater for human use. Part of this is returned after use and subsequently reused or left in nature.

water withdrawn water diverted from streams or rivers and pumped from groundwater aquifers for human use.

wetland a natural area covered at least part of the time or seasonally with water, such as a marsh, a floodplain, mudflats, or a delta.

World Water Commission established by the World Water Council to guide the World Water Vision exercise.

World Water Council established in 1996 as a neutral, nonprofit, nonpolitical, and independent forum to advocate, assist, and advise on global water issues—a global water policy think tank.

World Water Vision exercise the process developed for the World Water Vision with the participation of more than 15,000 people in an 18-month period.

Bibliography

Abramovitz, J.N. 1996. "Imperiled Water, Impoverished Future: The Decline of Freshwater Ecosystems." Worldwatch Paper 128. Worldwatch Institute, Washington, D.C.

Agarwal, A. 1999. Personal communication. Centre for Science and Environment, New Dehli, India.

Alaerts, G.J. 1999. "Institutions for River Basin Management: The Role of External Support Agencies (International Donors) in Developing Cooperative Arrangements." Paper presented at the International Workshop on River Basin Management: Best Management Practices, Delft University of Technology–River Basin Administration Centre, 27–29 October, The Hague.

Alcamo, J., and T. Henrichs, T. Roesch. 1999. "World Water in 2025: Global Modeling and Scenario Analysis for the World Commission on Water for the 21st Century." University of Kassel, Center for Environmental Systems Research, Germany.

Alcamo, J., P. Döll, F. Kaspar, and S. Siebert. 1997. "Global Change and Global Scenarios of Water Use and Availability: An Application of WaterGAP 1.0." University of Kassel, Center for Environmental Systems Research, Germany.

Ali, S.H. 1999. "Water Scarcity and Institutional Reform in Southern Africa." Water International 24(2): 116–25.

Allan, J.A., and J.H. Court, eds. 1996. Water, Peace and the Middle East: Negotiating Resources in the Jordan Basin. London and New York: Tauris Academic Studies.

Arriëns, W.L., J. Bird, J. Berkoff, and P. Mosley, eds. 1996. Towards Effective Water Policy in the Asian and Pacific Region: Overview of Issues and Recommendations. Proceedings of the Regional Consultation Workshop. Vol. 1. Manila: Asian Development Bank.

Australian Academy of Technological Sciences and Engineering and Australia Institutions of Engineers. 1999. Water and the Australian Economy. Victoria: Australian Academy of Technological Sciences and Engineering.

Ball, P. 1999. H_2O: A Biography of Water. London: Weidenfeld & Nicolson.

Barbier, E.B., and J.R. Thompson. 1998. "The Value of Water: Floodplain versus Large-scale Irrigation Benefits in Northern Nigeria." Ambio 27(6): 434–40.

Barraque, B. 1998. "Water Rights and Administration in Europe." In F.N. Correia, ed., Selected Issues in Water Resources Management in Europe. Eurowater Volume 2. Rotterdam: Balkema.

Bastidas, E.P. 1999. "Gender Issues and Women's Participation in Irrigated Agriculture: The Case of Two Private Irrigation Canals in Carchi, Ecuador." Research Report 31. International Water Management Institute, Colombo, Sri Lanka.

Berkoff, J. 1994. A Strategy for Managing Water in the Middle East and North Africa. Washington, D.C.: World Bank.

Bhatia, R., R. Cestti, and J. Winpenny. 1995. Policies for Water Conservation and Reallocation. Washington, D.C.: World Bank.

Bhatia, R., P. Rogers, and R. de Silva. 1999. "Water Is an Economic Good: How to Use Prices to Promote Equity, Efficiency, and Sustainability." TAC Working Paper. Global Water Partnership, Stockholm, Sweden.

Bingham, G., A. Wolf, and T. Wohlgenant. 1994. Resolving Water Disputes: Conflict and Cooperation in the United States, the Near East, and Asia. Irrigation Support Project for Asia and the Near East. Washington, D.C.: U.S. Agency for International Development.

Biswas, A.K. 1995. "Institutional Arrangements for International Cooperation in Water Resources." International Journal for Water Resources Development 11(2): 139–46.

Biswas, A.T., J. Kolars, M. Murakami, J. Waterbury, and A. Wolf. 1997. Core and Periphery: A Comprehensive Approach to Middle Eastern Water. Oxford: Oxford University Press.

Blokland, M., O. Braadbaart, and K. Schwartz, eds. 1999. Private Business, Public Owners: Government Shareholdings in Water Enterprises. The Hague: Ministry of Housing, Spatial Planning and the Environment.

Briscoe, J. 1997. "Managing Water As an Economic Good: Role for Reforms." Keynote paper at the International Commission on Irrigation and Drainage Conference on Water As an Economic Good, Oxford.

Brown, L.R., M. Renner, and B. Halweil. 1999. Vital Signs 1999–2000: The Environmental Trends that Are Shaping our Future. London: Earthscan Publications for Worldwatch Institute.

Bibliography

Bukar, M. 1999. "Water Resources Management Strategy Development in Nigeria." Paper presented at the African Water Resources Management Policy Conference, 26–28 May, Nairobi, Kenya.

Burrows, B., A. Mayne, and P. Newbury. 1991. *Into the 21st Century: A Handbook for a Sustainable Future.* Twickenham, U.K.: Adamantine.

Calder, I.R. 1998. "Water-Resource and Land-Use Issues." SWIM Paper 3. International Water Management Institute, Colombo, Sri Lanka.

Cestti, R., R. Bhatia, and C. van der Berg. 1994. "Water Demand Management and Pollution Control in the Jabotabek Region, Indonesia." World Bank, Washington, D.C.

Charrier, B., and P. Samson. 1997. *International Freshwater Conflict: Issues and Prevention Strategies.* Geneva: Green Cross International.

Chenje, M., and P. Johnson, eds. 1996. *Water in Southern Africa.* Maseru/Harare: Southern Africa Research and Documentation Centre, World Conservation Union, and Southern Africa Development Community.

Clarke, R.A. 1996. "Floods: Is Forecasting a Solution?" Paper presented at the International Association for Hydraulic Research and Engineering Southern African Division Biennial Congress "From Flood to Drought." 5–7 August, Sun City, South Africa.

Conway, G. 1999a. "Biotechnology, Food and Drought." Paper prepared for the World Water Commission. Rockefeller Foundation, New York.

———. 1999b. *The Doubly Green Revolution: Food for All in the 21st Century.* London: Penguin Books.

Correia, F.N. 1999. "Water Resources in the Mediterranean Region." *Water International* 24(1): 22–30.

———, ed. 1998a. *Institutions for Water Resources Management in Europe.* Eurowater Volume 1. Rotterdam: Balkema.

———. 1998b. *Selected Issues in Water Resources Management in Europe.* Eurowater Volume 2. Rotterdam: Balkema.

Correia, F.N., and J.E. da Silva. 1999. "International Framework for the Management of Transboundary Water Resources." *Water International* 24(2): 86–94.

Correia, FN., Y.Rees, E.B. Neves, B. Barraque, R.A. Kraemer, P.Perdok, and T. Zabel. 1998. "Overview of Water Availability, Uses and Institutions." In F.N. Correia, ed., *Institutions for Water Resources Management in Europe.* Eurowater Volume 1. Rotterdam: Balkema.

Cosgrove, W.J., and F.R. Rijsberman. 1998. "Creating a Vision for Water, Life and the Environment." *Water Policy* 1: 115–22.

———. 1999. "World Water Vision: Workplan 1999–2000." World Water Commission Water Vision Unit, Paris.

Costanza, R. 1997. "The Value of the World's Ecosystem Services." *Nature* 15 (May).

Department of Water Affairs and Forestry. 1997. "White Paper on a National Water Policy for South Africa." Pretoria, South Africa.

De Sherbinin, A., and V. Dompka. 1998. "Water and Population Dynamics: Case Studies and Policy Implications." American Association for the Advancement of Science, Program on Population and Sustainable Development, Washington, D.C.

Dinar, A. 1998. "Water Policy Reforms: Information Needs and Implementation Obstacles." *Water Policy* 1(4): 367–82.

Dinar, A., and A. Subramaniam. 1998. "Policy Implications from Water Pricing Experiences in Various Countries." *Water Policy* 1(2): 239–50.

Djerrari, M., and J.G. Janssens. 1999. "The Water Utility Partnership for Capacity Building in Africa." In G.J. Alaerts, F.J.A. Hartvelt, and F.M. Patorni, eds., *Water Sector Capacity Building: Concepts and Instruments.* Rotterdam: Balkema.

Easter, K.W., G. Feder, G. Le Moigne, and A.M. Duda. 1993. *Water Resources Management: A World Bank Policy Paper.* Washington, D.C.: World Bank.

EBRD (European Bank for Reconstruction and Development). 1999. *Municipal and Environmental Infrastructure.* London.

EC (European Commission). 1998. *Towards Sustainable Water Resources Management: A Strategic Approach.* Luxembourg: Office for Official Publications of the European Communities.

Elkaduwa, W.K.B., and R. Sakthivadivel. 1999. "Use of Historical Data As a Decision Support Tool in Watershed Management: A Case Study of the Upper Nilwala Basin in Sri Lanka." Research Report 26. International Water Management Institute, Colombo, Sri Lanka.

Esrey, S., J. Gough, D. Rapaport, R. Sawyer, M. Simpson-Hebert, J. Vargas, and U. Winblad, eds. 1997. *Ecological Sanitation.* Stockholm: Swedish International Development Authority.

EU (European Union), EIB (European Investment Bank), and World Bank. 1999. "MENA/MED Water Initiative Second Regional Seminar on Policy Reforms in Water Resources Management." Summary Report, 8–11 May, Amman, Jordan.

Falkenmark, M. 1998. "Dilemma When Entering the 21st Century: Rapid Change but Lack of a Sense of Urgency." *Water Policy* 1(4): 421–36.

———. 1999. "A Land-use Decision Is Also a Water Decision." In M. Falkenmark, L. Andersson, R. Castensson, and K. Sundblad, eds., *Water a Reflection of Land Use: Options for Counteracting Land and Water Mismanagement.* Stockholm: Swedish Natural Science Research Council and United Nations Educational, Scientific, and Cultural Organization–International Hydrological Programme.

Falkenmark, M., J. Lundqvist, and C. Widstrand. 1989. "Macro-scale Water Scarcity Requires Micro-scale Approaches: Aspects of Vulnerability in Semi-arid Development." *Natural Resources Forum* 1(4): 258–67.

Falkenmark, M., L. Andersson, R. Castensson, and K. Sundblad. 1999. *Water a Reflection of Land Use: Options for Counteracting Land and Water Mismanagement.* Stockholm: Swedish Natural Science Research Council and United Nations Educational, Scientific, and Cultural Organization–International Hydrological Programme.

Fall, A.F. 1999. "Strategie de gestion integree des ressources en eau au Senegal." Paper presented at the African Water Resources Management Policy Conference, 26–28 May, Nairobi, Kenya.

FAO (Food and Agriculture Organization). 1996. *Food Production: The Critical Role of Water.* Advanced ed. Rome.

———. 1999. "Irrigated Harvested Cereal Area for Developing Countries." Preliminary data. Rome.

Federal Interagency Stream Restoration Working Group. 1998. *Stream Corridor Restoration: Principles, Processes, and Practices.* Washington, D.C.: U.S. Department of Agriculture.

Foster, S., A. Lawrence, and B. Morris. 1998. *Groundwater in Urban Development: Assessing Management Needs and Formulating Policy Strategies.* World Bank Technical Paper 390. Washington, D.C.

Gallopin, G., and F.R. Rijsberman. 1999. "Third Generation of 3 Global Level Scenarios: Business-as-Usual (BAU), Technology, Economy and the Private Sector (TEC), and Values and Lifestyles (VAL)." Paper prepared for the World Water Commission, Paris.

Garcia, L.E. 1997. "Integrated Water Resources Management Strategy Paper." Inter-American Development Bank, Washington, D.C.

Gleick, P.H. 1998. *The World's Water 1998–1999: The Biennial Report on Freshwater Resources.* Washington, D.C.: Island Press.

———. 1999. "Water Futures: A Review of Global Water Resources Projections." Paper prepared for the World Water Commission, Paris.

———, ed. 1993. *Water in Crisis: A Guide to the World's Fresh Water Resources.* Oxford: Oxford University Press.

Glenn, J., and T.J. Gordon, eds. 1998. *The Millennium Project 1998 State of the Future: Issues and Opportunities.* Washington, D.C.: American Council for the United Nations University.

Global Water Partnership. 2000. *Towards Water Security: A Framework for Action.* Report of the Framework for Action Unit. Stockholm.

Grenon, M., and M. Batisse. 1989. *Futures for the Mediterranean Basin: The Blue Plan.* Oxford. Oxford University Press.

Groombridge, B., and M. Jenkins. 1998. "Freshwater Biodiversity: A Preliminary Global Assessment." World Conservation Monitoring Centre Biodiversity Series 8. World Conservation Press, Cambridge, U.K.

Hamdy, A., and C. Lacirignola. 1999. "Mediterranean Water Resources: Major Challenges Towards the 21st Century." Mediterranean Agronomic Institute of Bari, Italy.

Hammond, A. 1998. *Which World: Scenarios for the 21st Century.* Washington, D.C.: Island Press.

Hannan-Anderson, C. 1995. *A Gender Perspective on Water Resources Management.* Stockholm: Swedish International Development Authority.

Hirji, R., F-M. Patorni, and D. Rubin, eds. 1996. *Integrated Water Resources Management in Kenya.* Proceedings of a World Bank seminar, 22–25 January, Nanyuki, Kenya.

Hoek, W. van der, F. Konradsen, and W.A. Jehangir. 1999. "Domestic Use of Irrigation Water: Health Hazard or Opportunity?" *Water Resources Development* 15(1/2): 107–19.

Hoekstra, A.Y. 1998. *Perspectives on Water: An Integrated Model-based Exploration of the Future.* Utrecht, the Netherlands: International Books.

Hofwegen, P., and M. Svendsen. 1999. "A Vision of Water for Food and Rural Development." CEMAGREF, DVWK, FAO, Wallingford, ICID, ILRI, IPTRID, McGill, Wageningen University, World Bank. Washington, D.C.

Hornung, B.R. 1992. "Qualitative Systems Analysis As a Tool for Development Studies." In R.F. Geye and J. Van der Zouwen, eds., *Dependence and Inequality: A Systems Approach to the Problems of Mexico and Other Developing Countries.* Oxford: Pergamon Press.

Bibliography

Horst, L. 1998. "The Dilemmas of Water Division: Considerations and Criteria for Irrigation System Design." International Water Management Institute, Colombo, Sri Lanka.

Howe, C.W. 1997. "Water Pricing: An Overview." Paper presented at the World Bank seminar on Pricing of Sanitation and Water Services, 18–19 February, Washington, D.C.

———. 1998. "Protecting Public Values under Tradable Water Permit Systems: Economic Efficiency and Equity Considerations." University of Colorado, Institute of Behavioral Science, Boulder, Colo.

Huisman, P., K. Wieriks, and J. de Jong. 1999. "Capacity Building on an International Level: Developing Cooperative Agreements among Water Users in the Rhine Basin and North Sea." In G.J. Alaerts, F.J.A. Hartvelt, and F.M. Patorni, eds., *Water Sector Capacity Building: Concepts and Instruments*. Rotterdam: Balkema.

ICOLD (International Commission on Large Dams). 1997. "ICOLD Position Paper on Dams and the Environment." Paris.

IDI (Infrastructure Development Institute). 1997. "Drought Conciliation and Water Rights: Japanese Experience." IDI Water Series 1. IDI-Japan, Ministry of Construction, River Bureau, Tokyo.

IETC (International Environmental Technology Centre). 1996. *International Shiga Forum on Technology for Water Management in the 21st Century*. IETC Report 4. Shiga, Japan.

IFRC (International Federation of Red Cross and Red Crescent Societies). 1999. *World Disasters Report 1999*. Geneva.

IHA (International Hydropower Association). 1999. *Dams and Energy: Hydropower As the Preferred Alternative*. Geneva.

IJC (International Joint Commission). 1997. *The IJC and the 21st Century*. Washington, D.C.

Independent Commission on Population and Quality of Life. 1996. *Caring for the Future: Making the Next Decades Provide a Life Worth Living*. Oxford: Oxford University Press.

IPCC (Intergovernmental Panel on Climate Change). 1992. *1992 IPCC Supplement*. Geneva: World Meteorological Organization.

IRC (International Water and Sanitation Centre). 1995. *Water and Sanitation for All: A World Priority*. Ministry of Housing, Spatial Planning and the Environment, The Hague.

IUCN (World Conservation Union). 1999. "Vision for Water and Nature: Freshwater and Related Ecosystems—The Source of Life and the Responsibility of All." Version 4.1. Montreal, Canada.

IWMI (International Water Management Institute). 2000. *Water Supply and Demand in 2025*. Colombo, Sri Lanka.

Jansens, J.G. 1999. "Private Sector Participation Options in the Water Supply and Sewerage Sector." In G.J. Alaerts, F.J.A. Hartvelt, and F.M. Patorni, eds., *Water Sector Capacity Building: Concepts and Instruments*. Rotterdam: Balkema.

Jordans, E., and M. Zwarteveen. 1997. "A Well of One's Own: Gender Analysis of an Irrigation Program in Bangladesh." International Water Management Institute, Colombo, Sri Lanka.

Keller, A., R. Sahktivadivel, and D. Seckler. 1999. "Water Scarcity and the Role of Storage in Development." International Water Management Institute Discussion Paper. Colombo, Sri Lanka.

Kloezen, W.H. 1998. "Water Markets between Mexican Water User Associations." *Water Policy* 1(4): 437–55.

Koppen, B. van. 1998. "More Jobs per Drop: Targeting Irrigation towards Poor Women and Men." Ph.D. thesis. Wageningen University, Wageningen, the Netherlands.

———. 1999a. "More Crops and Jobs per Drop: Managing Water for Gendered Poverty Alleviation and Agricultural Growth." International Water Management Institute, Colombo, Sri Lanka.

———. 1999b. "Sharing the Last Drop: Water Scarcity, Irrigation and Gendered Poverty Eradication." Gatekeeper Series 85. International Institute for Environment and Development, London.

Kottelat, M., and T. Whitten. 1996. *Freshwater Biodiversity in Asia with Special Reference to Fish*. World Bank Technical Paper 343. Washington, D.C.

Kulshreshtha, S.N. 1998. "A Global Outlook for Water Resources to the Year 2025." *Water Resources Management* 12(3): 167–84.

Laredo, D., T. Selim, and J. Carney. 1999. "Development of Institutional Performance Indicators for the Water and Wastewater Sector in Egypt." In G.J. Alaerts, F.J.A. Hartvelt, and F.M. Patorni, eds., *Water Sector Capacity Building: Concepts and Instruments*. Rotterdam: Balkema.

Lecornu, J. 1998. "Dams and Water Management." Paper presented at the Ministry of Environment's International Conference on Water and Sustainable Development, 19–21 March, Paris.

Lemmelä, R., and N. Helenius, eds. 1998. *The Second International Conference on Climate and Water.* Espoo, Finland: IPPC.

Leonard, H.J. 1989. "Overview: Environment and the Poor." In H.J. Leonard, ed., *Environment and the Poor: Development Strategies for a Common Agenda.* Washington, D.C.: Overseas Development Council.

Lincklaen Arriens, W. 1999. "Towards Effective Water Policy in the Asian and Pacific Region: The Regional Water Policy Consultations of the Asian Development Bank." In G.J. Alaerts, F.J.A. Hartvelt, and F.M. Patorni, eds., *Water Sector Capacity Building: Concepts and Instruments.* Rotterdam: Balkema.

Lyonnaise des Eaux. 1998. *Alternative Solutions for Water Supply and Sanitation in Areas with Limited Financial Resources.* Nanterre, France.

Madramootoo, C.A. 1999. "The Vision for Canada's Water for the 21st Century: A Contribution Towards the Vision for World Water, Life and the Environment for the Twenty-first Century." McGill University, Quebec, Canada.

Mageed, Y.A., and G.F. White. 1995. "Critical Analysis of Existing Institutional Arrangements." *International Journal for Water Resources Development* 11(2): 139–46.

Malano, H.M., and P.J.M. van Hofwegen. 1999. *Management of Irrigation and Drainage Systems: A Service Approach.* International Institute for Infrastructure, Hydraulics and Environmental Engineering Monograph 3. Rotterdam: Balkema.

Mayur, R. 1996. *Earth, Man and Future: For the Renaissance Men and Women of the New Millennium.* Mumbai, India: International Institute for Sustainable Future.

McAllister, D.E., A.L. Hamilton, and B. Harvey. 1997. *Global Freshwater Biodiversity: Striving for the Integrity of Freshwater Ecosystems.*

Merrey, D.J. 1997. "Expanding the Frontiers of Irrigation Management Research." International Water Management Institute, Colombo, Sri Lanka.

Murunweni, Z. 1999. "Zimbabwe National Water Authority: Legislative Arrangements and Financing of Catchment Councils." Paper presented at the African Water Resources Management Policy Conference, 26–28 May, Nairobi, Kenya.

North, D.C. 1990. *Institutions, Institutional Change and Economic Performance.* Cambridge, U.K.: Cambridge University Press.

Odendaal, P.E. 1999. "The Sustainability of Urban Sanitation: Securing Human Health through Integrated Management and Capacity Building." Paper presented at the Stockholm Water Symposium, August, Stockholm.

OECD (Organisation for Economic Co-operation and Development). 1999. *Pricing of Water Services: An Update.* Paris.

Ongley, E.D. 1999. "Water Quality Management: Design, Financing and Sustainability Considerations." Paper presented at the African Water Resources Management Policy Conference, 26–28 May, Nairobi, Kenya.

Pazvakavambwa, S.C. 1999. "Addressing Historically Skewed Water Rights Arrangements: Water Resources Development Strategy in Zimbabwe." Paper presented at the African Water Resources Management Policy Conference, 26–28 May, Nairobi, Kenya.

Perry, C.J., and S.G. Narayanamurthy. 1998. "Farmer Response to Rationed and Uncertain Irrigation Supplies." Research Report 24. International Water Management Institute, Colombo, Sri Lanka.

Pinstrup-Andersen, P., R. Pandya-Lorch, and M.W. Rosegrant. 1999. *World Food Prospects: Critical Issues for the Early Twenty-first Century.* Food Policy Report. Washington, D.C.: International Food Policy Research Institute.

Postel, S. 1996. *Dividing the Waters: Food Security, Ecosystem Health and the New Politics of Scarcity.* Washington, D.C.: Worldwatch Institute.

———. 1999. *Pillar of Sand: Can the Irrigation Miracle Last?* New York: Norton.

Postel, S., and S. Carpenter. 1997. "Freshwater Ecosystem Services." In G.C. Daily, ed., *Nature's Services.* Washington, D.C.: Island Press.

Programme Solidarité Eau. 1998a. *Eau potable et assainissement: Dans les quartiers périurbains et les petits centres.* Paris: Cooperation Française.

———. 1998b. *Water and Sustainable Development: Experiences from Civil Society.* Paris: Cooperation Française.

Ramsar Convention Bureau. 1997. *The Ramsar Convention Manual: A Guide to the Convention on Wetlands (Ramsar, Iran, 1971).* 2nd ed. Gland, Switzerland.

Bibliography

Rangeley, R., B.C. Thiam, R.A. Andersen, and C.A. Lyle. 1994. *International River Basin Organizations in Sub-Saharan Africa.* World Bank Technical Paper 250. Washington, D.C.

Raskin, P., E. Hansen, and R. Margolis. 1995. "Water and Sustainability: A Global Outlook." Polestar Series Report 4. Stockholm Environment Institute, Sweden.

Raskin, P., M. Chadwick, T. Jackson, and G. Leach. 1996. "The Sustainability Transition: Beyond Conventional Development." Stockholm Environment Institute, Sweden.

Raskin, P., C. Heaps, J. Sieber, and G. Pontius. 1996. "Polestar Systems Manual: A Tool for Sustainability Studies." Stockholm Environment Institute, Sweden.

Raskin, P., G. Gallopin, P. Gutman, A. Hammond, and R. Swart. 1998. "Bending the Curve: Toward Global Sustainability." Polestar Series Report 8. Stockholm Environment Institute, Sweden.

Rees, J. 1998. "Regulation and Private Participation in the Water and Sanitation Sector." TAC Background Paper 1. Global Water Partnership, Stockholm, Sweden.

Rees, Y., T. Zabel, and J. Buckland. 1998. *Overview of Water Resources Management Issues.* In F.N. Correia, ed., *Selected Issues in Water Resources Management in Europe.* Eurowater Volume 2. Rotterdam: Balkema.

Revenga, C., S. Murray, J. Abramovitz, and A. Hammond. 1998. *Watersheds of the World: Ecological Value and Vulnerability.* Washington, D.C.: World Resources Institute and Worldwatch Institute.

Rijsberman, F. R., ed. 2000. *World Water Scenarios: Analysis.* London: Earthscan (forthcoming).

Rijsberman, F. R., and S. Westmacott. 1997. "Use of Decision Support Tools for Coastal Zone Managment in Curaçao and Jamaica." In *Integrated Water Resources Management for the Caribbean.* Trinidad: Caribbean Council for Science and Technology.

Rogers, P. 1998. "Should There Be an Industrial Water Policy." *Water Resources Update* 111: 46–51.

Rogers, P., R. Bhatia, and A. Huber. 1998. "Water As a Social and Economic Good: How to Put the Principle into Practice." TAC Working Paper. Global Water Partnership, Stockholm, Sweden.

Rosegrant, M.W., and P.L. Pingali. 1994. "Policy and Technology for Rice Productivity Growth in Asia." *Journal of International Development* 6(6): 665–88.

Rosegrant, M.W., and C. Ringler. 1999. *World Water Vision Scenarios: Consequences for Food Supply, Demand, Trade, and Food Security: Results from the IMPACT Implementation of the World Water Vision Scenarios.* Washington, D.C.: International Food Policy Research Institute.

Rosegrant, M.W., M. Agcaoili-Sombilla, and N.D. Perez. 1995. *Global Food Projections to 2020: Implications for Investment.* Washington, D.C.: International Food Policy Research Institute.

Saleth, R.M., and A. Dinar. 1998. "Water Institutions and Water Sector Performance: Evaluating Their Linkages with Cross-country Data." World Bank, Washington, D.C.

———. 1999. "Water Challenge and Institutional Response: A Cross-country Perspective." Policy Research Working Paper 2045. World Bank, Washington, D.C.

Salman, S.M.A. 1992. *The Legal Framework for Water Users' Associations: A Comparative Study.* World Bank Technical Paper 360. Washington, D.C.

———. 1999. "Water Users' Associations: Regulatory Framework for African Practice." Paper presented at the African Water Resources Management Policy Conference, 26–28 May, Nairobi, Kenya.

Salman, S.M.A., and L. B. de Chazournes, eds. 1998. *International Watercourses: Enhancing Cooperation and Managing Conflict.* World Bank Technical Paper 414. Washington, D.C.

SARDC (Southern Africa Research and Documentation Centre), IUCN (World Conservation Union), and SADC (Southern Africa Development Community). 1994. *State of the Environment in Southern Africa.* Harare, Zimbabwe: SARDC.

Schwartz, P. 1991. *The Art of the Long View.* New York: Doubleday.

Seckler, D., U. Amarasinghe, D. Molden, R. de Silva, and R. Barker. 1998. "World Water Demand and Supply, 1990 to 2025: Scenarios and Issues." Research Report 19. International Water Management Institute, Colombo, Sri Lanka.

Sharma, N.P., T. Damhaug, E. Gilgan-Hunt, D. Grey, V. Okaru, and D. Rothberg. 1996. *African Water Resources: Challenges and Opportunities for Sustainable Development.* World Bank Technical Paper 331. Washington, D.C.

Shiklomanov, I.A. 1998. *World Water Resources: A New Appraisal and Assessment for the 21st Century.* International Hydrological Programme report. Paris: United Nations Educational, Scientific, and Cultural Organization.

———. 1999. "World Water Resources and Water Use: Present Assessment and Outlook for 2025." State Hydrological Institute, St. Petersburg, Russia.

———, ed. 1997. "Assessment of Water Resources and Water Availability in the World: Comprehensive Assessment of the Freshwater Resources of the World." Stockholm Environment Institute, Sweden.

SIDA (Swedish International Development Authority). 1997. *Handbook for Mainstreaming a Gender Perspective in the Water Resources Management Sector.* Stockholm.

Sissay, A.S. 1999. "Water Resources Policy Strategy/Development in Ethiopia." Paper presented at the African Water Resources Management Policy Conference, 26–28 May, Nairobi, Kenya.

Smout, I., and S. Parry-Jones, eds. 1999. "Lessons Learned from NGO Experiences in the Water and Sanitation Sector." Loughborough University, Water, Engineering, and Development Centre, Leicestershire, U.K.

Sokolov, V.I. 1999. "Integrated Water Resources Management in the Republic of Uzbekistan." *Water International* 24(2): 104–15.

Solanes, M., and F.G. Villareal. 1999. *A Comparative Assessment of Institutional and Legal Arrangements for Integrated Water Management.* In G.J. Alaerts, F.J.A. Hartvelt, and F.M. Patorni, eds., *Water Sector Capacity Building: Concepts and Instruments.* Rotterdam: Balkema.

Stakhiv, E.Z. 1998. "Policy Implications of Climate Change Impacts on Water Resources Management." *Water Policy* 1(2): 159–75.

Strzepek, K. 1999. "Disaggregation of the World Water Vision Scenario Drivers for 18 regions with Polestar." Paper prepared for the World Water Commission, Paris.

Sundblad, K. 1999. "Regional Challenges." In M. Falkenmark, L. Andersson, R. Castensson, and K. Sundblad, eds., *Water a Reflection of Land Use: Options for Counteracting Land and Water Mismanagement.* Stockholm: Swedish Natural Science Research Council and United Nations Educational, Scientific, and Cultural Organization–International Hydrological Programme.

Svendsen, M., and M.W. Rosegrant. 1994. "Irrigation Development in Southeast Asia beyond 2000: Will the Future Be Like the Past?" *Water International* 19(1): 25–35.

Toth, F.I., E. Hizsnyik, and W. Clark, eds. 1989. *Scenarios of Socioeconomic Development for Studies of Global Environmental Change: A Critical Review.* Laxenburg, Austria: International Institute for Applied Systems Analysis.

UNCHS (United Nations Centre for Human Settlements). 1997. "Partnership in the Water Sector for Cities in Africa." Report of the Cape Town Consultations, 8–10 December, Cape Town, South Africa.

———. 1999. *Managing Water for African Cities.* UNCHS and United Nations Environment Programme Joint Initiative Project. Nairobi, Kenya.

UNDP (United Nations Development Programme). 1995. *Human Development Report 1995.* New York: Oxford University Press.

———. 1998. *Human Development Report Statistical Database.* Human Development Report Office, New York.

———. 1999. *Human Development Report 1999.* New York: Oxford University Press.

UNEP (United Nations Environment Programme). 1996. *Groundwater: A Threatened Resource.* UNEP Environment Library 15. Nairobi, Kenya.

———. 1999. *Global Environment Outlook 2000.* London: Earthscan Publications.

UNESCO (United Nations Educational, Scientific, and Cultural Organization). 1996. *Elles et l'Eau (Women and Water).* International Hydrological Programme–REUNIR Proceedings. Paris.

———. 1997. "Helping Children in the Humid Tropics: Water Education." Humid Tropics Programme Series 11. International Hydrological Programme, Paris.

———. 1998. *Water: A Looming Crisis?* Proceedings of the International Hydrological Programme's International Conference on World Water Resources at the Beginning of the 21st Century. Paris.

UNICEF (United Nations Children's Fund). 1998. *The State of the World's Children 1998.* New York: Oxford University Press.

United Nations. 1990. *Global Outlook 2000: An Economic, Social and Environmental Perspective.* New York: Earthscan.

Bibliography

———. 1999. *World Population Prospects: 1998 Revision*. New York.

United StatesCE (U.S. Army Corps of Engineers). 1999. *New Directions in Water Resources Planning for the U.S. Army Corps of Engineers*. Washington, D.C.: National Academy Press.

USDE (Unit of Sustainable Development and Environment). 1998. "Status and Proposed Actions to Continue the Implementation of the Initiatives on Water Resources and Coastal Areas of the Plan of Action for the Sustainable Development of the Americas." Report of the Inter-American Technical Meeting on Water, 8–9 December, Washington, D.C.

USEPA (U.S. Environmental Protection Agency). 1996. *Protecting Natural Wetlands: A Guide to Stormwater Best Management Practices*. Office of Water (4502F), Washington, D.C.

Van der Beken, A., ed. 1999. *A Guide to the Needs of Education and Training in the Water Sector*. Vrije Universiteit Brussel, ETNET, Belgium.

Vermillion, D.L., and C. Garcés-Restrepo. 1998. "Impacts of Colombia's Current Irrigation Management Transfer Program." Research Report 25. International Water Management Institute, Colombo, Sri Lanka.

Villiers, M. de. 1999. *Water*. Toronto, Canada: Stoddart Publishing.

Wakeman, W. 1995. *Gender Issues Sourcebook for Water and Sanitation Projects*. Washington, D.C.: United Nations Development Programme–World Bank Water and Sanitation Program, Water Supply and Sanitation Collaborative Council, Working Group on Gender Issues.

Ward, F.A., and P. King. 1998. "Reducing Institutional Barriers to Water Conservation." *Water Policy* 1(4): 411–20.

WARM (Water Resources Management Study). 1998. "Ghana's Water Resources: Management Challenges and Opportunities." Ghana Ministry of Works and Housing, Accra.

WBCSD (World Business Council for Sustainable Development). 1998. *Industry, Fresh Water and Sustainable Development*. Geneva.

Webb, P., and M. Iskandarani. 1998. "Water Insecurity and the Poor: Issues and Research Needs." Discussion Paper on Development Policy. Zeff, Bonn, Germany.

WFEO (World Federation of Engineering Associations). 1998. *Water Financing: The Engineers' Report on Water Privatization Projects in the Developing World*. Washington, D.C.

White, D.H., and L. Karssies. 1999. "Australia's National Drought Policy: Aims, Analyses and Implementation." *Water International* 24(1): 2–9.

White, W.R. 1999. "Water in Rivers: Flooding." Paper prepared for the World Water Commission on behalf of the International Association for Hydraulic Research and Engineering, Paris.

Whittington, D., D. Lauria, and X. Mu. 1989. "Paying for Urban Services." Report 1NU 40. World Bank, Washington, D.C.

WHO (World Health Organization). 1996. *Water Supply and Sanitation Sector Monitoring Report*. Geneva.

———. 1999. *World Health Report 1999*. Geneva.

Wijk, C. van, E. de Lange, and D. Saunders. 1998. "Gender Aspects in the Management of Water Resources." *Natural Resources Forum* 20(2): 91–103. International Water and Sanitation Centre, The Hague.

Wolf, A.T. 1998. "Conflict and Cooperation along International Waterways." *Water Policy* 1(2): 251–65.

———. 1999. "The Transboundary Freshwater Dispute Database Project." *Water International* 24(2): 160–63.

World Commission on Environment and Development. 1987. *Our Common Future*. Oxford: Oxford University Press.

WMO (World Meteorological Organization) and UNESCO (United Nations Educational, Scientific, and Cultural Organization). 1997. *Water Resources Assessment: Handbook for Review of National Capabilities*. Geneva.

World Bank. 1998. *World Development Indicators 1998*. Washington, D.C.

———. 1999. *World Development Report 1999/2000: Entering the 21st Century*. New York: Oxford University Press.

World Water Council. 1998a. *Long Term Vision for Water, Life and the Environment: A Proposed Framework*. Marseilles, France.

———. 1998b. *Water in the 21st Century*. Marseilles, France.

WRI (World Resources Institute), IUCN (World Conservation Union), and UNEP (United Nations Environment Programme). 1992. *Global Biodiversity Strategy: Guidelines for Action to Save, Study, and Use Earth's Biotic Wealth Sustainably and Equitably*. Washington, D.C.

WRI (World Resources Institute), UNEP (United Nations Environment Programme), UNDP (United Nations Development Programme), and World Bank. 1998. *World Resources 1998–99: A Guide to the Global Environment*. New York: Oxford University Press.

Wright, A.M. 1997. *Toward a Strategic Sanitation Approach: Improving the Sustainability of Urban Sanitation in Developing Countries.* Washington, D.C.: United Nations Development Programme–World Bank Water and Sanitation Program.

WSSCC (Water Supply and Sanitation Collaborative Council). 1997. *Water and Sanitation for All: Calling all Stakeholders.* Fourth Global Forum Proceedings and Manila Action Programme Report. Manila.

———. 1999. "Vision 21: A Shared Vision for Water Supply, Sanitation and Hygiene and a Framework for Future Action." Geneva.

WTO (World Tourism Organisation) and WMO (World Meteorological Organization). 1998. *Handbook on Natural Disaster Reduction in Tourist Areas.* Madrid.

WWF (World Wide Fund for Nature). 1998. *Living Planet Report.* Gland, Switzerland.

———. 1999. "A Place for Dams in the 21st Century" Discussion Paper. Gland, Switzerland.

Zwarteveen, M. 1997. "A Plot of One's Own: Gender Relations and Irrigated Land Allocation Policies in Burkina Faso." Research Report 10. International Water Management Institute, Colombo, Sri Lanka.

Index

Index

Index

World Water Council

Les Docks de la Joilette
10 Place de la Joilette
Atrium 10.3
1334 Marseille Cedex 2
France

Phone: +33 4 91 99 41 00
Fax: +33 4 91 99 41 01

Board of Governors, 1997–2000

President
Dr. Mahmoud Abu-Zeid, Ministry of Water Resources and Irrigation, Egypt

Vice Presidents
René Coulomb, Suez-Lyonnaise des Eaux, France
Aly M. Shady, Canadian International Development Agency, Canada

Treasurer
I. Najjar, HYDROSULT Inc., Canada

Chair, Finance Committee
Olcay Unver, Southeastern Anatolia Project, Turkey

Executive Director, ex officio
Jamil K. Al-Alawi

Chair, World Fund for Water
Pierre-Frédéric Ténière-Buchot, Agence de l'Eau Seine-Normandie, France

Chair, Regional Centres Committee
C.D. Thatte, International Commission on Irrigation and Drainage

Chair, Publications and Information Committee
Andras Szöllösi-Nagy, United Nations Educational, Scientific, and Cultural Organization

Chair, By-Laws Committee
Jacques Lecornu, International Commission on Large Dams

Chair, Program Committee
Roberto Lenton, United Nations Development Programme

Members

Mohamed Ait-Kadi, Ministère de l'Agriculture, du Developpement Rural et des Peches Maritimes, Morocco
Ger Ardon, Ministry for Housing, Spatial Planning, and the Environment, The Netherlands
Arthur Askew, World Meteorological Organization
Asit K. Biswas, Third World Center for Water Management, Mexico
Mohamed Ben Blidia, Institut Méditerranéen de l'Eau, France
Benedito Braga, International Water Resources Association
John D'Aniello, U.S. Army Corps of Engineers Civil Works, United States
Jean-François Donzier, Office International de l'Eau, France
Jean-Claude Gaudin, Ville de Marseille, France
Atef Hamdy, Istituto Agronomico Mediterraneo, CIHEAM, Italy
Kathryn Jackson, Tennessee Valley Authority, United States
Abbasgholi Jahani, Ministry of Energy, Iran
Mohamed Jellali, Ministère des Travaux Publics, Morocco
Richard Jolly, Water Supply and Sanitation Collaborative Council
Raymond Lafitte, International Hydropower Association
Richard Megank, Organization of American States
Malcolm Mercer, World Conservation Union
Tony Milburn, International Association on Water Quality
Miraji O.Y. Msuya, Nile Basin Initiative–TECCONILE, Uganda
John Pigram, Center for Water Policy Research, Australia
John Rodda, International Association of Hydrologic Science
Ismail Serageldin, World Bank
Michael Slipper, International Water Supply Association
Nicholas Sonntag, Stockholm Environment Institute, Sweden
Yukata Takahasi, Construction Project Consultants, Japan
C.V.J. Varma, Central Board of Irrigation and Power, India
Hongyuan Yuan, Wuhan University of Hydraulic and Electrical Engineering, China